Becoming a
Reflective Educator

John W. Brubacher
Charles W. Case
Timothy G. Reagan

Becoming a
Reflective Educator

*How to Build a
Culture of Inquiry
in the Schools*

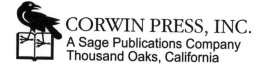

CORWIN PRESS, INC.
A Sage Publications Company
Thousand Oaks, California

For information address:

Corwin Press, Inc.
A Sage Publications Company
2455 Teller Road
Thousand Oaks, California 91320

SAGE Publications Ltd.
6 Bonhill Street
London EC2A 4PU
United Kingdom

SAGE Publications India Pvt. Ltd.
M-32 Market
Greater Kailash I
New Delhi 110 048 India

Printed in the United States of America

Library of Congress Cataloging-in-Publication Data

Brubacher, John W.
   Becoming a reflective educator : how to build a culture of inquiry in the schools / John W. Brubacher, Charles W. Case, Timothy G. Reagan.
      p.   cm.
   Includes bibliographical references and index.
   ISBN 0-8039-6094-8 (cl.)   — ISBN 0-8039-6095-6 (pbk.)
   1. Teaching. 2. Teaching—Case studies. 3. Teachers—Case studies. 4. School management and organization—Case studies. 5. Inquiry (Theory of knowledge). I. Case, Charles W. II. Reagan, Timothy G. III. Title
LB1027.5.3.B78   1994
371.1'02—dc20   93-27065

95 96 97 10 9 8 7 6 5 4 3 2

Corwin Press Production Editor: Rebecca Holland

Contents

Acknowledgments

For permission to reprint copyrighted material the authors gratefully acknowledge the following:

Clark, E. (1983, October). The Curious Odyssey of Dr. Littkey. *Yankee Magazine, 47*(10), 198-217.

Accelerated Schools Project. (1991). Hollibrook Accelerated Elementary School. *Accelerated Schools, 1*(3), 4-9.

Preface

Becoming a Reflective Educator is designed for use in teacher education programs that are devoted to the ideal of "reflective practice," as well as in advanced courses for experienced educators concerned with becoming more reflective in their teaching. The book—which seeks to combine case studies with discussions of various central themes related to teaching, professionalism, and reflective practice —has been carefully constructed to allow it to function as either the central textbook in a general introductory or foundational course in a teacher education program, or as a supplementary text in other courses (including the student teaching experience or advanced, graduate-level course work). Each chapter in *Becoming a Reflective Educator* begins with one or more case studies, which are then analyzed and discussed in terms of the chapter's focus. These cases provide the foundation on which the content of the chapter is then explicitly articulated and laid out. Finally, each chapter ends with a series of propositions, which are derived from the content of the chapter and offer points for further reflection and discussion.

The first chapter of the book offers a broad overview of the nature and purposes of "reflective practice" as such practice applies to the classroom teacher, as well as an explanation of how reflective practice differs from "good teaching," and an indication of what is entailed in the process of becoming a reflective practitioner. This chapter is central to the remainder of the book, and provides the organizing framework for the book.

Chapter 2 provides a general discussion of the role of inquiry in reflective practice; the general point of this chapter is that a necessary component of reflective practice is the ongoing commitment to inquiry, broadly conceived. The concept of inquiry developed in this chapter is based in large part on that discussed by the American philosopher of education, John Dewey, earlier in this century, and is expanded to include various qualitative and naturalistic approaches to inquiry as well as traditional understandings of what constitutes research. The chapter also seeks to build further on the concept of inquiry by focusing its attention on the ideal of the "teacher as researcher." It is argued in this chapter that the reflective, analytic teacher must also be a creative and innovative agent in the process of inquiry, and further, that the focus of such inquiry needs to be grounded in real-world problems and concerns that affect classroom teaching and learning. Finally, it is emphasized that there is no single approach to research or inquiry, and that the reflective practitioner must be open to a wide range and variety of inquiry options.

Chapter 3 offers an extended discussion of the nature, purposes, and objectives of transformational curricula and instruction. The theme of this chapter is that the development of such transformational curricula and instructional approaches is an essential aspect of reflective practice and must be undertaken in the same manner as other components of reflective practice. The likelihood of resistance to such innovation is also stressed in this chapter.

Chapter 4 addresses issues of leadership and followership in the school context, with special emphasis on the role of the reflective practitioner as an educational leader and follower. Implications of the themes of reflective practice and the culture of inquiry for school leadership are discussed, and the distinctions between and among transactional leadership, transformational leadership, and moral leadership are clarified.

The relationship between the school and the community is the subject of Chapter 5. The potential role of the school in preserving the status quo, or in advocating social change, is discussed through the use of case studies. The underlying theme of this chapter is that the schools are only one of a number of important social institutions, and that meaningful change in a democratic society necessitates that schools work together with a variety of other social institutions to achieve their ends.

Chapter 6 offers a broad overview of the role of professional ethics in reflective practice. After several case studies, the chapter presents a discussion of the differences among opinions, preferences, and value judgments, and then goes on to explore different ethical theories and their implications for teaching practice. The chapter concludes with a discussion of the role of reflection on ethical professional practice.

Finally, Chapter 7 offers some suggested activities that we believe will help individuals become more reflective and analytic professionals.

Becoming a Reflective Educator is the result of several years of collaboration at The University of Connecticut. During the past 5 years, the teacher education program at UConn has been radically transformed from a fairly traditional program, which consisted of a standard collection of courses topped off with a student teaching experience, to an innovative, 5-year program (2 years spent in general liberal arts course work, followed by 3 in the School of Education) that combines university course work, discussion seminars, and clinical and internship experiences throughout the 3 years of the teacher education program. The program is an integrated one in a number of ways; not only are university courses, seminars, and clinical experiences closely integrated, but so are the university courses themselves. Further, the program itself is an "integrated bachelor's/ master's program." As the faculty, students, and public school constituencies involved in this transformation have worked together to create an exciting and effective teacher education program, we have also reflected on our work and the program, and have continued to make changes as appropriate.

One of the underlying themes of the UConn teacher education program has been that we want to educate teachers who will themselves be "reflective practitioners." This book is the result of extended discussion among the three authors about how this could be accomplished. We see this book as a "manual" of sorts to help teacher education students as well as experienced teachers develop not only an understanding of the nature of "reflective practice," but also the attitudes and skills that such an approach to teaching requires.

Although *Becoming a Reflective Educator* is very much a collaborative effort, in most cases a single author has taken primary responsibility for writing specific chapters. John Brubacher is the primary author for Chapters 4 and 5, Charles Case is the primary author for Chapter 3, and Timothy Reagan is the primary author for Chapters 1 and 6. Chapter 2 was written collaboratively by Charles Case and Timothy Reagan, and Chapter 7 was written collaboratively by all three of the authors.

This book is our effort to help our students and others in their striving to become reflective practitioners. We hope that it is useful and successful, and would certainly appreciate comments, feedback, and suggestions for changes.

J. B.
C. C.
T. R.

About the Authors

John W. Brubacher is Professor Emeritus of Educational Administration at The University of Connecticut. For the past 23 years, he has been in the Department of Educational Leadership, where he served for 15 years as chairperson. Prior to becoming a professor, he was superintendent of schools in the Bellevue Public Schools in Bellevue, Washington, and in the Alpena Public Schools in Alpena, Michigan. He has also been an elementary school principal and classroom teacher. He was awarded an A.B. from Yale University; an M.A. from Teachers College, Columbia University; and a Ph.D. from the University of Michigan.

Charles W. Case is Dean of the School of Education, and Professor of Educational Administration, at The University of Connecticut. The author of more than 35 books, chapters, and articles dealing with various educational topics, he has actively championed both school reform and the reform of teacher education programs. A former public school teacher, he has also held appointments at the University of Iowa, the University of Wisconsin-Oshkosh, Cleveland State University, and the University of Vermont.

Timothy G. Reagan is Associate Professor and Program Coordinator of Educational Studies in the Department of Educational Leadership at The University of Connecticut. His areas of interest include teacher education, the education of culturally and linguistically dominated groups, multicultural education, educational in non-Western settings, and the education of the deaf. He has published extensively, and his work has appeared in such journals as *Harvard Educational Review*, *Educational Theory*, *Educational Foundations*, *Sign Language Studies*, *Language Problems and Language Planning*, and *Journal of Research and Development in Education*.

Reflective Practice and the Teacher

Too many people think they are thinking when all they are doing is rearranging their prejudices.

William James

The First Day of School: Three Case Studies

The first day of the school year at Emerson Elementary School was a difficult one for all three of the new teachers in the building. Sam Sharp, Doris Gleb, and Amy Gilson had all graduated from Northern State University with good grades and strong recommendations the year before, and all three, despite the inevitable first-day nerves, had started the day with high hopes. By the end of that first day of school, though, each of the three was tired, disappointed, and depressed.

Sam Sharp's First Day

Sam had been assigned one of the three first grade classes at Emerson. He had student taught in a second grade class during the spring semester, and had thought that he was ready for his own class. In fact, toward the end of his student teaching experience, he found that he actually preferred to be left alone with the class, rather

1

than have his cooperating teacher in the room with him. He felt confident of his ability to handle the class on his own, and believed that he was already a very good teacher. Ten minutes into his first day alone, though, things had started going wrong. He had problems with everything from collecting lunch money (with Sara Jameson's money—mainly in pennies!—going all over the place) to repeatedly losing control of the class as the noise and activity levels rose well beyond what he thought were reasonable limits. When he finally got home, he collapsed in a chair and began recounting his horror stories to his girlfriend, Jennifer, who listened patiently and tried to be supportive. In retrospect, as he talked about the day's events, Sam began to feel better about the day, and he started to see some humor in it. He even chuckled as he remembered the pennies rolling off in all directions, his own comic efforts to catch them, and the kids' roars of laughter. He'd lost control early in the day, he realized, and that had set the tone for everything else that happened. The problem, he decided, was that he'd been taking himself too seriously. He'd do a better job tomorrow, he was sure, and decided that the best thing to do would be to start the day by joking with the class that after the first day, things had to get better.

Doris Gleb's First Day

Doris had also had a long and hard day down the hall, trying to get her sixth graders organized for the school year. Things had started out all right, but rapidly deteriorated as the students continually tested her authority. By lunchtime, Doris knew that she needed to regain control, so after lunch she threatened to keep the whole class after school if they didn't settle down and get to work. The class had not only not improved, it had gotten wilder and more out of control by the hour. By the time the final bell rang, though, Doris didn't have the energy to try to keep the class after school, and in any case, she knew that with the bus schedules it wasn't really possible to do so. As she drove home, she became angrier and angrier. The day had been a disaster—there was no doubt about that. But after all, it hadn't really been her fault. Her methods teachers had never really taught her how to regain control of a class, and besides, if the kids were this bad, the principal should have warned her in advance so that she could be ready for them. She was also irritated that Mrs. Edson, the other sixth grade teacher, hadn't bothered to come in to see if she needed any help. It seemed to her that this was the least an experienced teacher could do for a new-comer. As she got home, Doris decided that things at school would eventually work themselves out, and what she needed was to take her mind off the day. So, she fixed herself a sandwich and turned on the television, looking forward to a quiet and relaxing evening.

Amy Gilson's First Day

Amy had arrived at school early so that she could finish getting her classroom set up the way that she wanted it. The bulletin boards were colorful and well done, emphasizing several of the themes that she planned to focus on with her third graders. The desks were in neat, straight rows, and she had already put the textbooks out on each desk. That way, she thought, she could get right down to teaching and not waste any time on set-up and classroom organization. As her students arrived, though, they seemed to have other ideas. During the first hour of class, several of the boys began "accidental-ly" pushing the piles of books off their desks. This game ended only when Amy actually yelled at Dennis Smith, one of the instigators of the game—something she'd never thought she would have to do to get control of her class. By recess, the neat lines of desks had deteriorated into snake-like rows, and a number of the children had made deliberately circuitous trips to the back of the room to sharpen pencils (and, in the process, had managed to push the desks into even odder, and less regular, patterns). By the end of the day Amy had a terrible headache and wondered whether she really wanted to be a teacher after all. Before leaving the school, though, she took 15 minutes to write in the journal that she'd been keeping since her first field experience in a school while in college. Much to her own amazement and chagrin, Amy quickly listed seven major mistakes that she thought she had made during the day, and was fairly sure there were others she'd missed. Next to each mistake, she left room to write in other comments later. She took the journal home with her and, after taking a couple of aspirin and fixing a cup of herbal tea, sat down and reread what she'd written. Then, next to each comment, she added a way of correcting or avoiding each of the mistakes in the future. For instance, next to "Neat rows were a dumb idea; they were like waving a red flag to the kids," she wrote, "I'm going to put the desks together in groups of four (or maybe 6?—I should ask one of the older teachers about this) and see if that helps." She still felt bad about yelling at Dennis, and promised herself that tomorrow she'd make a point of praising him about something. As she got up and closed her journal, she decided that she still wanted to be a teacher, but that it was obviously going to be a lot harder than she'd expected.

Analysis and Discussion. The first-day experiences of Sam, Doris, and Amy are instructive not because they tell us about good or bad teaching, or about such issues as classroom management or instructional strategies, but rather because they provide us with three very different models of how teachers can (and do) reflect on and respond to their classroom experiences. All three of these new teachers had relatively unsuccessful experiences, and all three had to some extent engaged in poor teaching practice. These elements are common not only to Sam, Doris, and Amy, but also to all teachers. Everyone who has ever entered a classroom as a teacher has had failures and has made mistakes and, from time to time, has made questionable pedagogical judgments and engaged in inappropriate or ineffective teaching practice. There are good teachers and bad teachers, but no perfect teachers. The difference between good teachers and bad teachers has as much to do with what they do after the fact as it does with what happens in the classroom at a given point in time.

Consider our three novice teachers and how each dealt with his or her failures during the first day. Sam exhibited fairly traditional teacher behavior—he went home and relived the day by recounting what happened to his girlfriend. Spouses of teachers will readily affirm that this is a common behavioral pattern among even the most experienced and successful teachers. At the end of the school day, we want to share our successes ("Mary Smith finally got a perfect score on the spelling test. I'm so proud of the way she's been working.") and to have someone to commiserate with about our failures ("I just can't figure out how to get Jack to take his work more seriously; I feel like I'm talking to a brick wall sometimes."). In Sam's case, the discussion was obviously fairly successful, since he did in fact identify a problem in his own conduct (taking himself too seriously) and work out a plan of action for correcting the problem.

Doris' response to the day's events was very different from Sam's. She, too, realized that the day had not gone well. However, unlike Sam, who had accepted his own responsibility for what had taken place in his classroom, Doris instead chose to place blame on others. She implicitly blames the children, categorizing them as "bad kids," and explicitly blames her college instructors, the principal, and her colleague, Mrs. Edson. One of the hardest lessons for many of us to learn is to take responsibility for our own actions and recognize that we are responsible for whatever takes place in our classroom. This is a lesson, it would seem, that Doris has not yet learned. Having assigned blame to virtually everyone except herself, Doris then decides that the situation at school will ultimately sort itself out, and puts it out of her mind. In other words, Doris has really not tried to identify what actually went wrong, nor has she developed any plan of action to either correct it or improve the situation in the morning. Since she has not really reflected in a constructive way about what took place in her classroom, and since she is expecting things to simply sort themselves out without help, it is unlikely that Doris's teaching will improve without a significant change of attitude and behavior on her part.

Amy, the last of our three novice teachers, had clearly tried to ensure that her first day on the job would be a positive and successful experience. Her day, though, like those of Sam and Doris, had turned out otherwise. In fact, things had gone so badly that she had even lost her temper with a student and yelled at him in class. As she tried to make sense of what had gone wrong, Amy used a process similar to but more formal than that used by Sam—she used a journal to record the major events of the day, and then, a bit later, to reflect on those events and develop strategies for dealing with the problems she had identified.

The responses of these three new teachers can be categorized as falling along a *continuum of reflectivity*—that is, the ways in which Sam, Doris, and Amy responded to their first day on the job demonstrate different degrees and kinds of reflection. Doris has, in effect, refused to reflect critically on the day's events at all, exhibiting essentially nonreflective behavior. Sam did reflect on the day's events and, based on his reflection, devised a strategy for correcting or at least improving the situation. His reflection was informal, though, and might more accurately be described as a combination of emoting about how he felt and thinking about what had happened. Finally, Amy's response to her first day of teaching entailed active and deliberate reflection, which included both a brief written description of the day's major events and a critical analysis of and reflection upon those events, which in turn led her to formulate strategies for changing her behavior in the classroom. In other words, Amy's reflection was far more formal and elaborate than was that of Sam and, as a consequence, may in the long run prove to be more useful and effective.

The cases of Sam, Doris, and Amy are useful in helping us to begin conceptualizing the nature and manifestations of reflective practice, but they all focus solely on the emergence of reflective practice on the part of *new* teachers. But what about experienced classroom teachers? As teachers develop an experiential base, they are able to become reflective in ways (and perhaps about things) that a new teacher is not. We now turn to three case studies that provide examples of reflection and reflective practice in the world of experienced classroom teachers.

The Complexities of Teaching: Three Case Studies

Rethinking the Content of U.S. History

Mary O'Reilly has taught social studies at Shepstone High School for 4 years. She has always considered herself a good teacher and has had relatively few problems in the past. This year, though, has been different, in large part, Mary believes, because of the presence of a large number of African-American students who have been bused in to previously all-white Shepstone High as part of the court-ordered desegregation of the city. Especially troublesome for Mary has been her third period U.S. history class. This class consists of students in the vocational track at Shepstone High and includes 12 of the bused students out of a total class enrollment of 25. Although she has covered exactly the same material in this class as in her other three U.S. history classes, and has tried to do so in the same way in each class, the students in the third period class have consistently done less well on their quizzes and exams than have the students in her other classes. Furthermore, 11 of the 12 African-American students have been in the D to F range throughout the year. On a Friday in early December, a week before the scheduled midterm examination, the students in the third period class, led by Larry Jones, a tall African-American student who seems to have gained the respect of the other vocational students throughout the school, rebelled during class. They complained that the textbook was too difficult, that the class was boring and irrelevant, and that she was a racist who was only interested in "what a bunch of old, dead white people did." Taken aback by the challenge to her authority, Mary quickly recovered her poise and said that she would think over what the class had said. To fill up the remainder of the period, rather than returning to the lecture that she had planned for the day, she asked each student in the class to take out a sheet of paper and write down three things, relevant to a class in U.S. history, that they would like to learn about. She collected the sheets of paper at the end of the period and, unsure of what she should do, watched the kids head off for their next class.

In the teachers' lounge during her free period, she shared what had happened with Jim Bender, one of the vocational education teachers at Shepstone. Jim shook his head, commenting that Larry Jones was a troublemaker and that what Mary needed to do was regain control of the class on Monday and remind the kids who was in charge. As Jim got up to leave, he turned and said, "Actually, none of this should surprise any of us—what did we think would happen, once they started busing those black kids in here? They should've left well enough alone." At home that night, as she thought about what had taken place during third period, and about Jim's comments, she decided that while it would be easier to blame the kids and busing, maybe Larry and the others did have a point. She'd always assumed that every U.S. history class should basically be interchangeable with every other U.S. history class, but perhaps that wasn't really good teaching. If she could find ways to get kids more excited about American history, they'd work harder and end up learning more—that just made sense. And, if that meant includ-ing material about African-Americans in U.S. history, then so be it. On the other hand, Mary realized that she didn't really know anything about African-American history or, for that matter, any perspec-tives on U.S. history other than the ones that she had learned as a student in college. She decided that it was about time for her to fill in some of the gaps in her knowledge, using the questions that the kids had given her in class as a starting point. She could go to the public library on Saturday and get some basic material on African-American history, then early next week she could call her college adviser and see if he had any additional suggestions.

Mary pulled the papers out of her third period folder and began looking them over, though not with much real hope—after all, this class had been such a disappointment all year. Much to her surprise, the questions were for the most part serious ones, raising some important historical questions that demonstrated a far better under-standing of what they'd covered in class than Mary had expected. As she read over the students' questions, she reached a decision. Monday in class she would praise the students both for raising the issues with her and for their thoughtful questions. She would admit to not knowing much about African-American history and would ask them to help her learn more—they'd try to work together to discover what none of them knew. At that point, Mary got out a pad of paper and began sketching a time line and identifying objectives for the rest of the school year, excited and looking forward to Mon-day's third period class more than she had since the start of the year.

Reporting a Colleague

Jeremy Butler had been a math teacher at Eastmoor Junior High School since the dark ages, or at least so the students believed. Actual-ly, he'd come to Eastmoor 17 years ago, straight out of college, and had become a popular and well-respected teacher in the district. New teachers were especially fond of him since he was always free to provide information and insights about the kids, their families, problems and backgrounds, the town, and the often mysterious workings of the school system. All in all, Jeremy was satisfied with his life and happy to let things continue as they always had, at least until Adrian Gregg joined the faculty as an English teacher. Adrian had come to the district from the military, having served a hitch after college as an Army officer, but showed no signs of a "military" approach to teaching. He was open, relaxed, and friendly, and the kids clearly loved him. He also appeared to be a very effective classroom teacher, since the kids were continually talking about his classes and how much they enjoyed what they were studying. By winter vacation, it was hard to believe that Adrian hadn't been around for years, and Jeremy, like most of the faculty at Eastmoor, was delighted to have Adrian as a colleague.

During the winter vacation, Jeremy went out for a drink with friends to a local bar. He saw Adrian across the room and went over to greet him. Adrian had clearly had a bit too much to drink, but was delighted to see Jeremy and they chatted pleasantly about their respective vacation plans. Jeremy thought nothing of the chance encounter, until one day in early February when he stopped by Adrian's classroom early in the morning to drop off a notice about a forthcoming union meeting. Adrian wasn't in the room, so Jeremy went over to his desk and put the notice on it. As he was turning to leave, Jeremy noticed that underneath the desk was a half-full bottle of Scotch. Not wishing to intrude on Adrian's privacy, or to jump to unwarranted conclusions, Jeremy quickly left the room and decided not to mention what he'd seen to anyone. As the day progressed, though, Jeremy became increasing concerned about what he had seen. If Adrian really had a drinking problem, then he needed help. Besides, if something were to happen to a child in one of Adrian's classes because Adrian wasn't fully sober, Jeremy knew that he would never forgive himself. On the other hand, if the principal were to find out about Adrian having the bottle on the premises, let alone any suspicions about alcoholism, that would mean the end of a promising teaching career. Eastmoor was a conservative community, and a new teacher with a drinking problem would have virtually no chance of having his contract renewed—he might even be fired outright. Furthermore, Jeremy knew that it was district policy that any suspicions about conduct on the part of a teacher that might endanger students were to be reported without delay to the school principal. Under the circumstances, if he did not report what he had seen, he himself might be at risk. What should he do?

After weighing the pros and cons of the situation mentally for several hours at home that night, Jeremy finally picked up the telephone and called Adrian at home. Adrian answered, sounding less than coherent. Jeremy told Adrian that he needed to speak with him about a personal matter and asked him to stop by his classroom after school the next day. Adrian agreed and showed up at Jeremy's classroom door right on schedule. Jeremy asked Adrian to sit down, and told him about accidentally seeing the Scotch bottle and shared his concerns that Adrian might have a serious drinking problem. Adrian admitted that he drank heavily, but denied having a drinking problem. He promised not to bring liquor into the school again, which he agreed had been a terrible mistake, and begged Jeremy not to report him. Jeremy asked Adrian to at least attend one meeting of Alcoholics Anonymous, but Adrian refused, arguing again that he really didn't have a problem, and besides, that Eastmoor was a small town and if he attended an AA meeting, word would get out and his career would be in jeopardy. Jeremy told Adrian that he'd think about the situation and let him know first thing in the morning what he'd decided to do.

It was the hardest decision Jeremy had to make since first becoming a teacher at Eastmoor. He really liked Adrian and believed that he was potentially an outstanding teacher. He also believed that Adrian was scared of the implications of his conduct, and thought that perhaps the concern for losing his job might lead to Adrian addressing his drinking. Jeremy didn't want to be responsible for the chance that Adrian might be fired. On the other hand, though, Jeremy recognized in Adrian's denial one of the classic behaviors of the alcoholic, and wondered whether Adrian could deal with his problem without professional help. Finally, Jeremy decided that his professional obligations to the students, to the district, and even to Adrian required that he discuss the matter with the school principal. He also decided, though, that he would make a strong case for retaining Adrian as long as he agreed to get professional help. After all his years in the system, he felt fairly certain that the principal would listen to him. It was the best that he could do, Jeremy decided sadly.

A Case of Child Abuse?

Juan Rodriguez was an experienced, skilled teacher who, after teaching fifth grade at West Springfield Elementary School for 7 years, still found it as exciting and challenging as he had when he first student taught. He enjoyed his time in the classroom and felt that he was having a positive effect on his students' development. He considered himself a good teacher and role model for his students and was confident that others in the school saw him as a caring and competent professional educator. The year had gone well, Juan thought to himself one morning in April, as he watched the children working in small groups throughout the room on their social studies projects. Then he noticed the bruises on the back of Jennifer Gordon's left leg. Jennifer had become one of Juan's favorite students; bright, articulate and attractive, she was a friendly and outgoing girl whose mother was actively involved in the school PTO as well as a variety of local community groups, and was well known and liked by many of the school faculty. Juan had no reason at all to suspect that there were any problems in Jennifer's home life, but felt that in keeping with the school district's policy of reporting all cases of child abuse, he really did need to find out the source of Jennifer's bruises. Not wishing to create a disturbance or upset Jennifer, Juan waited until recess and, while outside on the playground with the children, caught her attention and engaged her in conversation. Jennifer seemed to be very nervous about answering Juan's questions about the bruises, and quickly responded that she'd fallen off her bike. Sensing her nervousness, Juan dropped the subject and let her return to play with the other children. He had, he realized, a real moral dilemma: Reporting a case of suspected child abuse automatically involved the police, and the Gordons were respected citizens in the community. He really didn't have any hard evidence and, while Jennifer was clearly nervous about discussing the bruises, that didn't necessarily mean that she'd been physically harmed by her parents. Deciding to give the matter some thought before he did anything, Juan went home that night with the issue unresolved.

Juan arrived at school early the next morning, hoping to see Janet Clark, the reading consultant for the district and a good friend. Janet, in the office picking up her mail, greeted Juan with a ready smile. When he asked her to come down to his room to "talk something over," she agreed to come at once and followed him down the hall to his classroom. Juan shared with Janet what he had seen the day before and told her about Jennifer's reaction to his questions. Janet also thought that Jennifer's nervousness sounded odd, but she, too, knew the family's reputation and found it hard to believe that Jennifer's parents could be guilty of child abuse. After talking it over together, the two decided that the best thing would be to take it slow and easy, just observing Jennifer more closely the next few weeks to see if anything else suspicious took place. After all, children get bruises all the time, they agreed, and Jennifer's home life was by all accounts a good one. It would be a terrible thing for good parents to be accused of child abuse if they weren't guilty. Juan felt much better as Janet left, though he wasn't positive that they'd really made the right decision.

Analysis and Discussion. The three case studies you have just read present us with somewhat more difficult and complex examples of the kinds of dilemmas and problems inevitably faced by classroom teachers. Although dealing with very different kinds of issues, each of the experienced classroom teachers demonstrates a number of similar characteristics and behaviors. While one may disagree with the conclusions that each teacher reached, or with aspects of his or her behavior in the situation, it is nevertheless clear that all three teachers were in fact attempting to engage in reflective practice.

In the case of Mary O'Reilly's third period U.S. history class, students explicitly challenged the content of the curriculum and implicitly challenged the teaching methods that the teacher has been employing. Mary's experience as a classroom teacher can be seen clearly in her ability to temporarily defuse the tense classroom situation, as well as in her willingness to jettison her planned lesson in favor of a more appropriate alternative in the class. After the class is over, Mary discusses the situation with a colleague, though his advice, most of us would agree, is poor if not absolutely reprehensible. Mary appears to agree with this assessment upon reflection and ultimately, after a difficult but useful self-critique, decides to both admit that her students' concerns are legitimate and attempt to develop and implement a plan designed to address the student complaints. Throughout the experience Mary tries to take her students and their concerns seriously, though an element of patronage seems to exist as well in her responses. Mary could be faulted for not realizing the biased nature of the curriculum on her own, of course, and she still has not realized that her teaching methods as well as the content that she is teaching may be problematic. In short, this case demonstrates reflective practice related to such issues as curriculum and diversity on the part of an experienced classroom teacher, though we may have reservations or concerns about whether the practice exemplified actually constitutes "good" teaching. What is clear, though, is that Mary will continue to struggle and try to improve her teaching.

The case of Jeremy Butler and Adrian Gregg focuses not on classroom practice, but rather on professional ethics and on the educator's responsibility for and toward other professional educators, as well as toward the school district and children served by the district. The decision that Jeremy Butler is called upon by circumstances to make is difficult, and one may well disagree with the decision that he finally makes. However, as with Mary, what we see in Jeremy's behavior is a thoughtful, reasoned effort to reach a good judgment about what action he should take in the matter. We see him weighing the evidence and data and considering the situation in light of both its moral and practical consequences. It is clear that Jeremy cares deeply about both what happens to Adrian and what is best for the students. It is also interesting to note that Jeremy does not take what for many would be the easy way out: simply reporting his suspicions because the rules require it. Ethical behavior, whether personal or professional, requires that we do more than merely follow the rules blindly and unthinkingly, and Jeremy clearly understands this. On the other hand, perhaps due to the nature of the situation, Jeremy seeks to make his decision in a vacuum, without discussing his options with anyone else. The result of this is that he takes on far more personal responsibility in the matter than he really needs to, and may fail to identify other options that are available to him in dealing with the problem of Adrian's drinking.

The case of Juan Rodriguez and Jennifer Gordon will be for many of us the most difficult of the three to address. By virtue of our training, our predispositions, and our life-styles, good teachers generally tend to like and enjoy children and would not want to contribute to child abuse, even indirectly. On the other hand, we are also sensitive to the harm that a false charge of child abuse can cause. As in the case of Adrian Gregg, there are times when experienced teachers are likely to bend or break school rules, violate district policies, and even break laws when their judgment is that doing so is the "right" thing to do. In this particular case, after both trying (perhaps unsuccessfully) to find out from Jennifer what had happened and discussing the situation with a colleague, Juan decides not to report his suspicions. He has tried to weigh the evidence and his concerns and is obviously interested in protecting Jennifer. It is also evident that both Juan and Janet will now be attentive to any other indications of possible child abuse in Jennifer's case. On the other hand, both Juan and Janet seem to have been somewhat inhibited by the social standing of Jennifer's parents—it is not at all clear that Juan would have reached the same conclusion had another child with less well-known parents been involved.

The characteristic seeming to hold all three of these case studies together is that in each instance the teacher demonstrated an awareness of and concern with what Thomas Green has called the "conscience of craft" (Green, 1985, pp. 4-7). In a discussion of the formation of individual conscience (that is, of moral development) in contemporary society, Green suggests that:

> There is such a thing as the conscience of craft. We see it whenever the expert or the novice in any craft adopts the standards of that craft as his or her own. In other words, it is displayed whenever we become judge in our own case, saying that our performance is good or bad, skillful, fitting, or the like. . . . Thus, to possess a conscience of craft is to have acquired the capacity for self-congratulation or deep self-satisfaction at something well done, shame at slovenly work, and even embarrassment at carelessness. (p. 4)

In each case, the teacher was faced with a dilemma that she or he needed to resolve. Each dilemma required that the teacher utilize both professional knowledge (whether about the curriculum, professional ethics, or indicators of child abuse) and rational decision-making skills to make a judgment about and take action in response to the dilemma. Although one may have serious reservations (or even disagreements) with the decisions reached and actions taken by the three teachers in these cases, it is clear that each did his or her best to comply with Green's notion of the "conscience of craft," and further that each individual, regardless of the correctness or wrongness of his or her decision, decided what to do only after careful, thoughtful reflection. With these six case studies in mind, we can now turn to a more detailed discussion of what is actually entailed in *reflective practice,* and why such reflective practice is in fact a desirable goal for the classroom teacher.

The Nature of Reflective Practice

A perennial debate among educators and those interested in education has been about the nature of teaching. The debate is most commonly presented as a dichotomy, with the basic issue being defined as whether teaching is best understood as an artistic endeavor, with the teacher's role seen as roughly comparable to that of the painter or creative writer, or as a sort of "science," consisting of a collection of technical skills, where the role of the teacher is seen as having more in common with that of a medical technician or an automobile mechanic (see Barzun, 1954, 1991; Gage, 1978, 1985; Highet, 1950). At first glance, the debate appears to be an important one, since the way we conceptualize teaching has a great deal to do with whether teachers are seen (and, of course, rewarded) as professionals, such as doctors, lawyers, engineers and the like, as well as how teachers can best be prepared (can good teachers be made, or are they just "born," as the adage goes?). Writing in defense of the artistic view of the teacher, for instance, Mark Van Doren has commented that:

> Good teachers have always been and will always be, and there are good teachers now. The necessity henceforth is that fewer of them be accidents. The area of accident is reduced when there is a design which includes the education of teachers. Not the training—a contemporary term that

suggests lubricating oil and precision parts, not to say re-
flexes and responses. (Van Doren, 1959, pp. 170-171)

Although the debate between those who see teaching as basically an art form that is largely instinctive in good teachers and those
who see it as a scientific set of technical skills that virtually anyone,
properly motivated, can acquire, is a fascinating one to listen to and
think about, it is also to a very great extent misleading, much as the
nature/nurture debate is misleading. It is misleading because experienced educators know that teaching entails many elements of
both artistic sensitivity and technical skill, and that good teaching
practice is impossible without both types of elements. It is interesting to note that one could make precisely this same claim for the
competent practice of virtually all professions. For example, in considering what a physician actually does, one finds a combination of
technical skills and knowledge and professional "instinct" that is in
essence artistic in nature, which is remarkably similar to that exhibited by teachers. An excellent illustration of this point is provided
in *Newton's Madness: Further Tales of Clinical Neurology* (Kalwans, 1990),
a collection of case studies by a noted neurologist that read more
like a detective novel than a medical work. The underlying theme
in *Newton's Madness* is that medical diagnosis is actually far less
scientific (at least in a narrow, positivistic sense) than most of us
normally assume. The medical education that a doctor receives is
intended to help him or her identify possible diagnoses and eliminate
others, but very often the final diagnosis depends to a considerable
extent on judgment calls. This point was clearly recognized in the
1984 GPEP report of the Association of American Medical Colleges,
titled *Physicians for the Twenty-First Century*, which, according to the
medical historian Kenneth Ludmerer, went on to conclude: ". . . that
medical education should prepare students 'to learn throughout
their professional lives rather than simply to master current information and techniques.' To accomplish this, students must be active, independent learners and problem solvers rather than passible
recipients of information" (Ludmerer, 1985, p. 264). Furthermore,
critics of modern American medical practice often note that where
technical competence is removed from ethical and humanitarian
concerns, what is left is essentially poor medical practice and treat-

ment (see, for example, Jones, 1981). As Paul Starr has noted, "In its commitment to the preservation of life, medical care ironically has come to symbolize a prototypically modern form of torture, combining benevolence, indifference, and technical wizardry. Rather than engendering trust, technological medicine often raises anxieties about the ability of individuals to make choices for themselves" (Starr, 1982, p. 390).

It is the need to make such judgment calls that will, at least for the immediate future, limit the usefulness of computer diagnosis, for instance, since the computer can only perform the technical aspects of the physician's task. The artistic functions continue to require a human presence. The same is true for other professions as well (see Case, Lanier, & Miskel, 1986; Schön, 1983, 1987; for an interesting and relevant discussion of the training of attorneys, see Stevens, 1983), and is certainly true in the case of teaching. An interesting point here is that Ivan Illich, who is perhaps best known for the criticism of compulsory schooling he offered in *Deschooling Society* (1970), has also critiqued contemporary medical practice in roughly the same manner, based in large part on the similarities of the medical and educational establishments (see Illich, 1975; Reagan, 1980).

Much of the daily work of the classroom teacher actually involves making judgments and decisions, often with limited information. Rather than thinking about the role of the teacher in terms of whether teaching is best understood as an art form, a set of technical skills, or some combination of these two extremes, we would suggest that teaching can be more accurately and usefully conceptualized in terms of the role of the teacher as decision maker. Consider for a moment the many different kinds of judgments and decisions the typical teacher engages in during his or her normal, daily routine. The teacher makes curricular decisions; methodological decisions; decisions about individual children, their needs, and problems; decisions about classroom management and organization; decisions about both personal and professional ethics; and so on. The philosopher of education Robert Fitzgibbons has suggested that teachers make decisions of three types: those concerned basically with *educational outcomes* (that is, with what the goals or results of the educational experience should be); those concerned with the *matter of education* (that is, with what is, could be, or should be taught); and those concerned with the *manner of education* (that is, with how teaching should take place) (Fitzgibbons, 1981, pp. 13-14).

When a teacher makes decisions, she or he is doing far more than merely taking a course of action or acting in a certain way. The process of decision making should be a rational one, which means that the teacher (whether consciously or unconsciously) considers and weighs alternatives and employs criteria to select a given option or course of action. Unfortunately, as Jere Brophy has reported, "most studies of teachers' interactive decision-making portray it as more reactive than reflective, more intuitive than rational, and more routinized than conscious" (quoted in Irwin, 1987, p. 1). Good teaching, however, requires reflective, rational, and conscious decision making. As Charles E. Silberman (1971) argued in *Crisis in the Classroom*, "We must find ways of stimulating public school teachers . . . to think about what they are doing and why they are doing it" (p. 380). An important element in this process of reflective, rational, and conscious decision making is that we can reasonably expect a teacher to be able to justify his or her decisions and actions in the classroom. Justification of decisions and actions, as Cornel Hamm explains, is actually a fairly simple and straightforward matter: "To provide a justification for a course of action is to provide good reasons or grounds for that course of action" (Hamm, 1989, p. 163).

To be able to provide such justification, the teacher cannot rely either on instinct alone or on prepackaged sets of techniques. Instead, she or he must think about what is taking place, what the options are, and so on, in a critical, analytic way. In other words, the teacher must engage in *reflection* about his or her practice, just as the physician must reflect about the symptoms and other evidence presented by a patient. The idea of the teacher as reflective practitioner is not a new one; John Dewey, the noted American philosopher of education, wrote about the need for reflective thinking as early as 1903, and dealt with the role of reflection extensively in both *How We Think* (1910, 1933) and *Logic: The Theory of Inquiry* (1938). For Dewey, logical theory and analysis was a generalization of the reflective process in which we all engage from time to time. Dewey recognized that we can "reflect" on a whole host of things in the sense of merely "thinking about" them; however, logical, or *analytic*, reflection can take place only when there is a real problem to be solved. As Dewey explained:

> The general theory of reflection, as over against its concrete exercise, appears when occasions for reflection are so over-whelming and so mutually conflicting that specific ade-quate response in thought is blocked. Again, it shows itself when practical affairs are so multifarious, complicated, and remote from control that thinking is held off from successful passage into them. (Dewey, 1976, p. 300)

For Dewey, then, true reflective practice takes place only when the individual is faced with a real problem that he or she needs to resolve and seeks to resolve that problem in a rational manner. All three of our new teachers were faced with problems that they believed to be quite real and of considerable personal interest; both Sam and Amy engaged (although to different degrees and in different ways) in what Dewey would see as reflection.

Recent emphasis on the need for reflective practice comes large-ly from the work of Donald Schön (1983, 1987), which has been widely used by educators and others interested in the preparation of classroom teachers. Such concerns with reflective practice are also tied very closely to efforts to empower teachers, as Catherine Fosnot (1989) notes: "An empowered teacher is a reflective decision maker who finds joy in learning and in investigating the teaching/learning process—one who views learning as construction and teaching as a facilitating process to enhance and enrich develop-ment" (p. xi).

A number of different ways of conceptualizing reflective prac-tice, as it applies to the activities of classroom teachers, have been suggested in recent years. A good place to begin a discussion of reflective practice is with the distinction among the three types of reflection that Killion and Todnem (1991), using Schön's (1983) earlier work as a base, have suggested. According to Killion and Todnem (p. 15), we can distinguish among *reflection-on-practice, reflection-in-practice,* and *reflection-for-practice.* Both reflection-in-practice and reflection-on-practice are essentially reactive in nature, being distinguished primarily by *when* reflection takes place—with reflection-in-practice referring to reflection in the midst of practice (as in the case of Mary O'Reilly's change in her day's lesson as a result of her students' actions, or in the case of Juan Rodriguez's seeking to get information from Jennifer about her bruises on the playground); and reflection-on-practice referring to reflection that takes place after an event. Reflection-for-practice, on the other hand, as Killion and Todnem argue, is: "the desired outcome of both previous types of reflection. We undertake reflection, not so much to revisit the past or to become aware of the metacognitive process one is experiencing (both noble reasons in themselves), but to guide future action (the more practical purpose)" (p. 15).

In other words, reflection-for-practice is in essence proactive in nature. Examples of reflection-for-practice can be found in almost every case study presented in this chapter; only in the case of Doris Gleb is there no indication of reflection-for-practice. To sum up, it is clear that all three types of reflection discussed here will be necessary components of reflective practice on the part of the classroom teacher. Having said this, it is also important for us to note here that the relative significance of each of these three components of reflective practice may change over the course of an individual teacher's career; thus, for the novice teacher, reflection-for-practice and reflection-on-practice may be the most obvious ways in which his or her practice is distinguished; while for the expert or master teacher, reflectivity may be best seen in his or her reflection-in-practice. Further, the process of engaging in reflection-for-practice should be seen not as a linear one, but as an ongoing spiral in which each of the elements of reflective practice is constantly involved in an interactive process of change and development.

Van Manen (1977) has suggested a hierarchical model of *levels of reflectivity*. According to Van Manen, there are three distinct levels of reflective practice that can be seen, at least ideally, as paralleling the growth of the individual teacher from novice to expert or master teacher. The first level is concerned with the effective application of skills and technical knowledge in the classroom setting. At this first level, reflection entails only the appropriate selection and use of instructional strategies and the like in the classroom. The second level, according to Van Manen, involves reflection about the assumptions underlying specific classroom practices, as well as about the consequences of particular strategies, curricula, and so on. In other words, at the second level of reflectivity teachers would begin applying educational criteria to teaching practice to make individual and independent decisions about pedagogical matters. Finally, the third level of reflectivity (sometimes called *critical reflection*) entails the questioning of moral, ethical, and other types of normative criteria related directly and indirectly to the classroom. As Judith Irwin (1987) has explained:

> This includes concern for justice, equity and the satisfaction of important human purposes within the larger social context. A teacher engaging in this level of reflection, then, would be able to not only make decisions which would be beneficial for the long-term development of the students in that classroom but also to contribute to educational policy beyond his/her individual classroom. (p. 5)

Another approach to conceptualizing reflective practice is not to view such practice in an hierarchical manner, but rather to focus instead on elements that appear to play significant roles in fostering reflection and reflective practice on the part of classroom teachers. Georgea Sparks-Langer and Amy Colton, for instance, in a synthesis of the research on teachers' reflective thinking, have argued that there are three such elements: the *cognitive element,* the *critical element,* and the *narrative element* (Sparks-Langer & Colton, 1991). The *cognitive element* of reflective thinking is concerned with the knowledge that teachers need to make good decisions in and about the classroom situation. Lee Shulman has identified seven broad categories of knowledge that would, taken together, constitute the major categories of the knowledge base for a classroom teacher, and which are therefore necessary for successful, reflective teaching practice. These seven broad categories include:

- content knowledge;
- general pedagogical knowledge, with special reference to those broad principles and strategies of classroom management and organization that appear to transcend subject matter;

- curriculum knowledge, with particular grasp of the materials and programs that serve as "tools of the trade" for teachers;
- pedagogical content knowledge, that special amalgam of content and pedagogy that is uniquely the province of teachers, their own special form of professional understanding;
- knowledge of learners and their characteristics;
- knowledge of educational contexts, ranging from the workings of the group or classroom, the governance and financing of school districts, to the character of communities and cultures; and
- knowledge of educational ends, purposes, and values, and their philosophical and historical grounds. (Shulman, 1987, p. 54)

It is important to note that while all teachers, whether novice or expert, will have similar bodies of knowledge at their disposal, the organization and structuring of this knowledge may differ radically. Research conducted by cognitive psychologists has suggested that the *schemata*, or organized networks of facts, concepts, generalizations, and experiences, of beginning and experienced teachers are very different in significant ways (see Berliner, 1986; Sparks-Langer & Colton, 1991, pp. 37-38). Since such schemata are constructed by teachers over time as a result of their experiences, it is not surprising that experienced teachers will often be able to make sense of and respond to a given problematic situation in the classroom more quickly and effectively than would novices. Studies suggesting that expert teachers are able to deal with changes in lesson plans and problematic classroom situations far more successfully than are new teachers can be explained, according to Sparks-Langer and Colton, "because (1) many of the routines and the content were available [to the expert teachers] in memory as automatic scripts and (2) their rich schemata allowed the experts to quickly consider cues in the environment and access appropriate strategies" (1991, p. 38). *Schemata* of the sort discussed here are constructed naturally over time, of course, but their development can be encouraged and supported by reflective practice. In other words, while good teaching practice does indeed depend on a strong experiential base, reflective practice can help speed up the development of such an experiential base in new teachers.

The second element of reflective thinking, the *critical element*, is concerned with "the moral and ethical aspects of social compassion and justice" (Sparks-Langer & Colton, 1991, p. 39). Concerns with issues of social justice and ethics in education are and have been common to educators and educational theorists at least since Plato (see, for example, Chambliss, 1987), and are clearly manifested in such common and important distinctions made by educators as that between educational product goals (i.e., what we want to achieve in the classroom or the school) and process goals (i.e., the restrictions that exist on how our product goals can be achieved) (see Teal & Reagan, 1973).

The third element of reflective thinking, the *narrative element*, has to do with teachers' narratives. Teacher accounts of their own experiences in the classroom take many forms and serve a variety of different functions. Amy's journal is an example of one fairly common type of narrative. Other kinds of narrative discourse on the part of teachers include descriptions of critical events in the classroom, various types of logs and journals, conference reports completed jointly by teachers and supervisors or mentors, self-interviewing, and so on. The key aspect of the narrative element of reflective thinking is that such narratives, whatever their form, serve to contextualize the classroom experience, both for the teacher and for others, and consequently provide us with a much richer understanding of what takes place in the classroom and in the teacher's construction of reality than would otherwise be possible. Narrative accounts are becoming far more common today, especially in the preparation of teachers and in qualitative research on classroom practices (see Connelly & Clandinin, 1990; Goswami & Stillman, 1987; Zeichner & Liston, 1987), and there can be little doubt that they provide one of the most effective ways in which reflective practice can be encouraged.

A useful way of thinking about both the reflective teacher and the nature of the reflective practice in which he or she will engage has been provided by Judith Irwin (1987), who has suggested that:

A reflective/analytic teacher is one who makes teaching decisions on the basis of a conscious awareness and careful consideration of (1) the assumptions on which the decisions are based and (2) the technical, educational, and ethical consequences of those decisions. These decisions are made before, during and after teaching actions. In order to make these decisions, the reflective/analytic teacher must have an extensive knowledge of the content to be taught, pedagogical and theoretical options, characteristics of individual students, and the situational constraints in the classroom, school and society in which they work. (p. 6)

Notice that this description includes virtually all of the issues that have been discussed thus far. We see that the reflective teacher is first and foremost a decision maker, who must make his or her decisions consciously and rationally. Further, the reflective teacher must base his or her decisions and judgments on a solid body of content, including both technical and content knowledge, which are organized and reinterpreted according to his or her unique experiences. The reflective teacher must also demonstrate both ethical behavior and sensitivity as well as sociocultural awareness. As Case et al. (1986) note, "The attendant characteristics of professions include conditions of practice that allow professionals to apply this knowledge freely to the practical affairs of their occupation and to use their knowledge, judgment, and skill within the structures of the ethical code of the profession . . . "(p. 36). Finally, it is important to note that reflective practice involves what the teacher does before entering the classroom, in terms of his or her planning and preparation, for instance; while in the classroom, both while functioning as an educator and in all of the other roles expected of the classroom teacher; and retrospectively, after she or he has left the classroom.

Such a conceptualization of the reflective teacher makes clear how very much is being expected of the classroom teacher by advocates of reflective practice. Why, one might ask, should a teacher devote so much time and energy to becoming a reflective practitioner? What, in short, are the benefits of reflective practice? There are a number of benefits to be gained from reflective practice, including:

1. reflective practice helps to free teachers from impulsive, routine behavior;
2. reflective practice allows teachers to act in a deliberate, intentional manner; and
3. reflective practice distinguishes teachers as educated human beings since it is one of the hallmarks of intelligent action.

Further, as we have already noted, reflective practice is useful in helping to empower classroom teachers. Most important, though, reflective practice is a tool for individual teachers to improve their own teaching practice and to become better, more proficient, and more thoughtful professionals in their own right.

Becoming a Reflective Practitioner

The process of becoming a reflective practitioner, like that of becoming a "good teacher," is a long and, in many ways, difficult one. Becoming a reflective practitioner has much in common, in fact, with the process of becoming "real" as the Skin Horse explained it to the Rabbit in the children's story, *The Velveteen Rabbit* (Williams, 1981, pp. 14-16). Just as becoming "real" takes time, and happens after a toy has lost its hair and become shabby, so becoming a truly reflective teacher involves time, experience and, inevitably, a bit of wear around the edges. However, every teacher, at every stage of his or her career, can and should strive to become a reflective practitioner, knowing that only by making the effort to become reflective and analytic can one really be said to become a "good teacher," just as every toy knows that being loved by a child is the only way to become "real."

Propositions for Reflection and Consideration

1. The study of reflective thinking need not result in an individual becoming a reflective practitioner. To be become a reflective practitioner, a person must alter his or her behavior.
2. Reflective practitioners identify categories of knowledge that are requisite for successful reflective teaching (for example, content, pedagogy, curriculum, learning, educational contexts,

educational ends). They use these categories to analyze and modify practice.

3. Reflective practitioners are concerned and involved with issues of social justice and ethics in education.

4. Reflective practitioners make conscious, rational decisions based upon a solid and defensible knowledge base.

Toward a "Culture of Inquiry" in the School

Disinterested and impartial inquiry is then far from meaning that knowing is self-enclosed and irresponsible. It means that there is no particular end set up in advance so as to shut in the activities of observation, forming of ideas, and application. Inquiry is emancipated. It is encouraged to attend to every fact that is relevant to defining the problem or need, and to follow up every suggestion that promises a clue. The barriers to free inquiry are so many and so solid that mankind is to be congratulated that the very act of investigation is capable of itself becoming a delightful and absorbing pursuit, capable of enlisting on its side man's sporting instincts.

John Dewey (1948, p. 146)

Inquiry as a Component of Good Teaching: A Case Study

Janet Rivers has been a sixth grade teacher at Riverside Elementary School for 7 years. She is very popular with students, parents, and colleagues, and has a reputation for being an excellent, though strict, teacher. Janet has always tried to follow the advice that her cooperating teacher gave her when she student taught: never smile until Christmas. For Janet, this means that she spends the first half of the year ensuring that the children in her care know the classroom rules and the behavior that she expects from them, and she does this by posting the rules on a bulletin board in the front of her class, discussing each rule and the reasons behind the rule, and enforcing the rules without exception. This approach has always worked for Janet in the past; it is only this year that it has resulted in problems for her.

Billy Simons is a bright, pleasant child who has never had problems with any teacher before this year. Both his parents have been involved in PTO activities and have been cooperative and supportive of the school. According to the teachers who have had him in class in the past, Billy has been successful, both academically and socially, and has never had a significant conflict with a teacher. Almost from the very beginning of the current year, however, Billy and Janet Rivers have been engaged in repeated confrontations. Billy has persisted in questioning and challenging the rules that Janet has tried to enforce, and it has become increasingly difficult for her to deal with him in class.

At the first parent conference, Janet expressed her concerns about Billy's behavior to his parents, though she was also careful to assure them that his academic work did not appear to be affected. She was very surprised when Billy's mother told her that Billy spoke about her a great deal at home, and felt very frustrated because he believed that she disliked him and that nothing he could do would please her. Billy's father then noted that as far as he could tell, Billy's acting out in school was unique—his behavior at home had been fine, and neither his Sunday School teacher nor his Boy Scout leader had noted any similar problems.

Janet went home that night and could not get Billy out of her mind. She had a serious problem with this youngster, one that she had never encountered before, and she wanted to sort it out as soon as possible for everyone's sake. Billy's parents hadn't been at all hostile; indeed, at several points in the conference, his mother had seemed far more concerned about Janet's feelings than about Billy. She wasn't dealing with Billy effectively in class, and that, Janet decided, was the basic problem. Why was she having problems with Billy, when other teachers hadn't had similar problems? Regretfully, she realized that the only new variable in Billy's life was his teacher: She must be at the root of the problem. What was she doing that was so different from what had come before in Billy's school experience? As she thought about her colleagues, Janet noted to herself that she tended to be far stricter than the other teachers at Riverside. She believed in discipline and in enforcing her rules fairly and even-handedly, and had never been one to display much emotion in class. Perhaps, though, a middle ground was possible. She decided to try an experiment in class the next day.

Janet had decided to try using active praise of Billy as a way of modifying his behavior; rather than focusing on the situations that had caused conflict in the past, she decided, just for this one day, to comment only on the positive things that he did. At one point, when the children were supposed to be sitting at their desks working, Janet noticed that Billy was standing next to Sarah, quietly trying to explain a part of the worksheet that Sarah clearly didn't understand. Biting her tongue to stop her rebuke, Janet instead said, "Billy, that's very helpful—I really appreciate your helping Sarah. When you finish, though, would you sit back down and make sure you finish your own worksheet?" Billy looked up, a bit puzzled and perplexed, and Janet smiled at him. For the first time that year, Billy actually grinned back and said, "Yes ma'am," quickly finished with Sarah and sat down at his desk. Janet was astounded, because the situation had the makings of one of her standard arguments with Billy (Billy, sit down. But I was just helping. . . . Billy, I said sit down. You know the rules. And so on).

Driving home that night, Janet mentally reviewed what had taken place during the day. The class had gone very smoothly, with fewer hassles and problems than usual—in large part, she had to admit, because she and Billy hadn't been constantly at each other. Billy had responded very well to her whenever she praised him, and a smile seemed to go a long way in getting his cooperation. She wondered if perhaps she and her cooperating teacher could have been wrong, or at least whether the rule didn't work in Billy's case. She was still concerned about what the implications of her experiment were for her teaching methods generally. She couldn't treat children differently and still be fair, and yet there was no denying that a different approach seemed to work wonders for Billy. Janet decided to extend the experiment a bit longer, and to discuss the issue of fairness and same treatment with her friend Amy Shearson, a fourth grade teacher at Riverside, at the first opportunity.

Analysis and Discussion. The case that you have just read is an interesting one for a variety of reasons. It raises questions about teaching methods, about ethics (especially about the possible tension between effectiveness and fairness), and about reflection and its role in the classroom. Janet Rivers has been, by all accounts, a good teacher for a number of years. By the time that she has Billy Simons in her class, many of her classroom management behaviors have become habitual ones that she was used to employing without thinking about them. Such habitual behaviors are natural and often useful: There are many things that each of us does every day without reflection or active thought. For instance, in driving a car, when I come to a red light, I do not take time to think about the meaning of the light or make a thoughtful judgment to stop my car. Rather, I respond in a way that is essentially a conditioned response. Janet's habitual classroom behaviors, for which she has a theoretical rationale grounded in past experience, fail to achieve the desired results with Billy. Whatever one may think of Janet's philosophy of classroom management, it is at this point that she begins acting in the way one would expect a good teacher to respond. She is troubled and perplexed, and she subjects her habitual behavior to critical, reflective analysis.

In Janet's case, this reflective analysis results in the identification of the problem (her tried-and-true methods aren't working effectively in the case of Billy Simons), and the formulation and implementation of an alternative strategy. Finally, as the strategy is implemented, Janet engages in an ongoing evaluation of its effectiveness. Notice that this case is concerned with the type of problem situation that might easily arise in virtually any classroom, and further, that Janet's response to the problem situation involves nothing more complex or sophisticated than common sense and a willingness to try new things. Nevertheless, Janet's behavior in this situation provides us with a good example of Dewey's notion of "free inquiry."

Much classroom inquiry is of the informal sort illustrated in this case, but there is also considerable inquiry in classroom settings of a somewhat more formal sort. We turn now to several case studies in which different types of more formal inquiry is taking place in classroom settings.

Inquiry as Research: Four Case Studies

Albion Middle School is a large urban school with a culturally and linguistically diverse student body. This school is of particular interest to us because a variety of different kinds of formal inquiry-based activities are currently taking place here. Let's look at several of these activities now as examples of inquiry in the school context.

Reducing Mathematics Anxiety

A study of the effectiveness of an experimental mathematics anxiety reduction program is currently being conducted by Leslie Smith, a graduate student from the local state university, in Jim Andrews's eighth grade algebra classes. Leslie provided Jim with a set of prepackaged anxiety reduction activities for him to use in his third period class, and is using his fifth period class as a control group. The activities to be used with students include focused discussions about mathematics and fears of mathematics, role-playing activities in which mathematical knowledge must be applied to everyday problems, and so on (see Kogelman & Warren, 1978). The populations in the two classes were randomly assigned, and both classes contain roughly comparable populations. The study being conducted will use pre- and post-tests to determine the effectiveness of the anxiety reduction activities. When the data has been collected, Leslie will analyze it and write it up for her thesis at the university, and hopes to publish a research article about the experiment. Jim has been delighted to play a part in the research study, since he has been bothered by the problems caused by math anxiety among his students and hopes to learn how to better deal with the problem as a result of the study.

An Ethnographic Inquiry

A somewhat different kind of inquiry has been taking place in the English department, where Joan Richardson, a former teacher now enrolled in a doctoral program at a university in another state, is back and is engaged in what she calls an ethnographic study. She has been sitting in on various ninth grade English classes, taking notes and occasionally tape-recording classes. She has also been collecting class handouts and assignments, and spends a lot of time chatting with the English teachers about what they are trying to accomplish in their classes. She has also asked to read student essays and plans to interview students, both individually and in groups. She even team-teaches some classes with her former colleagues. Her goal, she says, is just to "understand what's happening in the English program"—not to make recommendations or predictions. Although they've been a bit puzzled by what exactly it is that she is trying to accomplish, Joan's former colleagues have enjoyed having her around again and appreciate the extra help she often provides in their classes. They've also noticed that she is very easy to talk to, a good person with whom they can talk over classroom problems.

Collaborative Research and the Science Curriculum

Jim Bowen, Jackie Lefevre, and Tanya O'Dell, the school's three science teachers, have been engaged in yet another type of inquiry. During the summer vacation, the three met several times to discuss ways in which they could improve the science learning of their students. All three had been concerned that students at Albion were just memorizing content without gaining any real understanding of the scientific principles that undergirded the science curriculum. As a result of their summer meetings, they agreed to try modifying both the curriculum and their teaching methods in the seventh grade general science classes that they all teach. During the current year, all three teachers have been trying to use more hands-on kinds of activities in their teaching, and have stressed that students need to *discover* scientific concepts and ideas rather than simply learning them. For example, rather than simply lecturing about the causes of volcanic eruptions, as he had done in the past, Jim divided his classes into teams of four to five students. Each team was given two quart-sized beakers and was told to fill one beaker with water and one with talcum powder. Jim then gave each team two straws, and had a selected student on each team put the straws into the beakers and blow into the straws. He then had the class discuss what had happened, and explained the similarity to different sorts of volcanic eruptions.

During the school year he three teachers have continued to meet twice a month, on a Saturday at a local diner, to discuss the progress and problems that each has had, and all three have tried to keep a daily log of issues that have come up in their classes and the ways in which they've tried to deal with them. They have found that by meeting outside the school setting, they feel freer to discuss problems and possible solutions, and have agreed that nothing that they share among themselves will be repeated at school. Some of the ideas that they began with in September have been abandoned, others have been modified, and the year has turned out very differently than they expected. In the case of the example given above, for instance, Jim decided afterwards that to reduce the huge mess in his classroom, next year he would have a single team conduct the volcano experiment in front of the class. None of the three believes that they've "gotten it completely right" yet, and there have been some really tough times when everything seemed to be going wrong, but on the whole their experience has been a positive one. None of the three teachers has any intention of publishing the results of their activities, nor are any using the experience for advanced degrees. They see themselves simply as teachers trying to improve their practice in a collaborative, supportive way.

Involving Students in Inquiry

Bill Jones has been teaching social studies at Albion since it opened 15 years ago. One of only a small number of African-American teachers in the district, Bill is widely acknowledged as an outstanding teacher whose enthusiasm for his subject is contagious for even the most "difficult" students. This year has been no exception. There has been a controversial debate in the county about the possible placement of a low-level nuclear waste facility near the town, and Bill and his eighth grade students have spent most of the year talking about and researching the debate. They have worked as a team, with Bill functioning mainly as a group facilitator, to find out as much as they could not only about the nature and risks posed by such a facility, but also about the policy-making process and how they could make their concerns heard. His students have spent a great deal of time in both the school and local public library, and have attended several town council meetings, as well as meetings of the local zoning board. Bill and his students even toured a nearby power station after the manager saw them at a zoning board meeting and invited them to see the plant in person. Bill readily admits that he knew almost nothing about nuclear power and nuclear waste facilities before the year started, and says that he and his students have really worked together to learn what they needed to know.

Analysis and Discussion. These four case studies are all concerned with the process of inquiry in a school context, but the nature and purposes of the inquiries, as well as the ways in which they are conducted and how one would evaluate them, are very different in many ways. In the first case study, we are presented with a fairly traditional research study, in which we can identify the dependent and independent variables, and in which there is a test group and a control group. The researcher in this study is seeking to be neutral and objective, and the subjects of the study are observed in terms of behavioral changes that occur as a result of planned activities designed to modify behavior. The second case is also a university-driven study, but the researcher is immersed in what she is studying and is in fact a participant in her own study. Further, while in the first study the researcher was presumably concerned with the generalizability of her results (that is, with the study's external validity), in the second case Joan is interested only in "understanding"—rejecting, it would seem, any concern with generalizability. The third case study presented a very different kind of inquiry; indeed, many people would say that only the first two cases, or perhaps even only the first, are really examples of educational research. What Jim Bowen, Jackie Lefevre, and Tanya O'Dell are engaging in is certainly different from the first two cases, and yet they too are trying to study their classes, engage in reflective problem solving, develop hypotheses, test their hypotheses, and so on. What is more, they are doing so *together*, both challenging and supporting one another as they come to understand and, hopefully, improve their teaching practice. Even more than in Joan Richardson's case, they are participants in their own study—in fact, in a way one could say that they and their behaviors in the classroom are one of the foci for their inquiry. The kind of inquiry in which these three science teachers are engaging is sometimes called the *teacher as researcher* model or approach. Last, in the fourth case study we see a teacher, Bill Jones, and his students working together on an issue of common concern. In this last case, the collaboration that characterized the three science teachers engaging in the process of teacher as researcher is taking place not among teachers, but between the teacher and his students. In short, the subjects have themselves become the researchers, and they are not only engaged in inquiry, but are also determining the nature, purposes, and direction of that inquiry.

As indicated earlier, many people would argue that not all the cases discussed above are really examples of research. The important point, for our purposes here, is not really whether these cases are all instances of research, though we believe that they are. Rather, the significant issue here is that all four cases demonstrate individuals trying to understand, in a more or less formal manner, some aspect of their world. While these four cases do differ in some very important ways, they also share a number of common features, and it is to a discussion of these shared features of the process of inquiry that we now turn.

The Concept of Inquiry

Yvonna Lincoln and Egon Guba, two well-known and respected qualitative researchers, begin their book, *Naturalistic Inquiry,* by commenting that:

The history of humankind is replete with instances of attempts to understand the world. Our curiosity has been directed at the same fundamental questions throughout time; our progress as inquirers can be charted by noting the various

efforts made to deal with those questions. What is the world?
How can we come to know it? How can we control it for our
purposes? What is, after all, the *truth* about these matters?
(Lincoln & Guba, 1985, p. 14)

This provides an excellent starting point for making sense of the
concept of inquiry. Basically, as the quote suggests, inquiry refers
to our attempts to understand and make sense of the world (or parts
of the world) around us. Inquiry can be more or less formal, more
or less rigorous, and involving a wide range of different techniques
and methods. The process of inquiry can even entail very different
(and sometimes incompatible) ideas and assumptions about the
nature of knowledge and knowing, and different individuals will
often approach the process of inquiry in quite different ways. Further, as Lincoln and Guba argue, inquiry is ultimately concerned with
a number of common fundamental issues. In education, for instance,
virtually all research and inquiry is ultimately concerned with the
improvement of teaching and learning. Having said this, of course,
it is also important to note that the focus of any specific inquiry will
be far narrower and concerned with only a small part of this broader
and more general issue. For example, we find inquiries concerned
with organizational matters, ethical matters, pedagogical matters,
curricular matters, and so on, all of which constitute perfectly appropriate educational inquiry. As all of this would suggest, there is
no single model of inquiry that includes all cases and types of
educational inquiry. There are, rather, many different models that
have been suggested to describe the inquiry process, and we will
now briefly examine a few of these models.

Perhaps the most common conceptualization of the inquiry process is what is somewhat misleadingly called the "scientific method."
This is a formalized description of the process in which scientists
(and especially those working in the physical sciences) are presumed
to engage as they try to discover new knowledge. The scientific
method can be broken down into five distinct steps: identification
of a problem, definition of the problem, formulation of hypotheses,
projection of consequences, and the testing of hypotheses (see
Fraenkel & Wallen, 1990, pp. 6-7). The goal of utilizing the scientific
method is to test ideas about the world in a formal, public, and

rigorous manner. Researchers who try to use the scientific method are attempting to ensure the neutrality and objectivity of their research and the results of their research; an underlying theme of the scientific method is that the researcher or inquirer should be irrelevant to the research or inquiry being conducted. Such a view exemplifies what is known as the *positivist* (or sometimes *post-positivist*) paradigm of educational research.

The utilization of the scientific method in conducting educational research is often appropriate and valuable. Much of what we know about aspects of good teaching and of student learning comes from research conducted in this way. The study being conducted at Albion Middle School on mathematics anxiety reduction by Leslie Smith is an example of inquiry based on the scientific method. There are some important limitations to research of this kind, however. Because of its underlying assumptions, research based on the scientific method excludes certain in-depth sorts of studies and inquiries, and inevitably underplays or rejects altogether the role of intuition in inquiry. In contrasting different approaches to educational inquiry, it is useful to consider a distinction suggested by the anthropologist Clifford Geertz, who distinguishes between two kinds of research: that which provides us with a *thin description* of a context, and that which gives us a *thick description* (Geertz, 1973, 1983). In order to obtain a thick description, the researcher or inquirer must been immersed in the context of the inquiry; indeed, it is often best if the researcher is actually a participant in the study (see Hammersley, 1990, 1992; Spradley, 1980; Whyte, 1991). The scientific method approach to inquiry can provide us with detailed information about the reading achievement of students in a third grade class, and can point out variables that correlate with increased achievement. An ethnographic study, however, could tell us a great deal more about the way in which students and teachers interact in that same third grade class, as well as help us understand how both the teacher and the students make sense of the classroom (that is, how each constructs his or her reality). The former type of inquiry would provide us with a thin description, the latter with a thick description. Both can be very useful in improving education; neither on its own gives us a complete picture.

The American philosopher of education, John Dewey, wrote extensively about the application of the scientific method to social and educational problems. Dewey, however, conceived of the scientific method in a somewhat broader way than that discussed above (see Sherman & Webb, 1988b, pp. 11-18). Rather than seeing inquiry as an activity set apart from normal, everyday life, Dewey believed that "inquiry is the life-blood of every science and is constantly engaged in every art, craft and profession" (Dewey, 1938, p. 4). Further, he recognized that "inquiry is a mode of activity that is socially conditioned and that has cultural consequences" (Dewey, 1938, p. 19), and that when we are engaged in the process of inquiry:

> In actual experience, there is never any . . . isolated singular object or event; *an* object or event is always a special part, phase, or aspect, of an environing experienced world—a situation. The singular object stands out conspicuously because of its especial focal and crucial position at a given time in determination of some problem of use or enjoyment which the *total* complex environment presents. There is always a *field* in which observation of *this* or *that* object or event occurs. (Dewey, 1938, p. 67)

In short, the approach to inquiry suggested by Dewey attempts to place inquiry and its objects in a social, and normative, context. In a discussion of Dewey's views on the process of inquiry, Henry Levin explains that:

> The inquiry approach is a systematic and disciplined method for understanding problems, finding and implementing solutions, and assessing their results. It is a process for incorporating values, obtaining information on alternatives, and building on the strengths and talents of staff, parents, and students. It is also an approach to testing solutions to see if they work. (Levin, 1991, p. 2)

The idea that it is necessary for us to contextualize our inquiry, and to view inquiry as a dynamic rather than as a static process, has provided the foundation for what is commonly known as *qualitative* or *naturalistic* inquiry. Studies that are qualitative or naturalistic in orientation are concerned with providing a thick description of a context (to use Geertz's terminology) and attempt to offer a holistic perspective of the social and cultural context in which they occur. An important facet of such inquiries is that they presuppose the existence of multiple, constructed realities rather than a single, objective reality. Thus, the point of Joan Richardson's study is in essence to understand how the teachers in the English program make sense of their world, and how the students in their classes make sense of the same classroom situations. To some extent, each individual in each classroom is engaged in constructing his or her own reality, and the goal of the researcher is to try to understand all of these different constructions of reality.

As the inquirer begins a naturalistic study, he or she necessarily becomes part of what is being studied. The researcher in a classroom is not invisible to the teacher and students, and his or her presence in the room (no matter how unobtrusive he or she attempts to be) does change the setting of the study. As a result of this, some researchers seek to make the best of this situation by becoming active participants in their own studies, as Joan Richardson did to a limited extent. When this takes place, we speak of *participant observation* types of research (Spradley, 1980). Further, on some occasions the inquiry is actually being conducted by the participants themselves for their own ends, as is the case with both the three science teachers and Bill Jones. Inquiry of this sort is called *action research,* since its primary objective is to improve practice (see Bissex & Bullock, 1987; Kemmis & McTaggart, 1988; Mohr & MacLean, 1987). What we are concerned with at this point, though, are not so much the different types of inquiry; rather, our concern is with the characteristics necessary for an individual to engage in inquiry.

In all four of the examples of inquiry taking place at Albion Middle School, the individuals involved share a number of characteristics that are central to the inquiry process. These individual characteristics are intellectual curiosity, motivation, openness in inquiry, and openness to challenge. Each of these characteristics will now be discussed briefly.

All inquiry is ultimately based on curiosity. Dewey (1933, pp. 36-39) suggests that there are three developmental stages of curiosity:

organic (or physiological) curiosity, of the sort one sees in a cat playing with a ball of string or in a toddler "getting into everything"; social curiosity, in which facts are sought from others (the "why?" stage of child development); and last, intellectual curiosity, which is characterized, in Dewey's words, by the transformation of curiosity "into interest in finding out for oneself the answers to questions that are aroused by contact with persons and things" (Dewey, 1933, p. 39). It is with the development and nurturing of intellectual curiosity that the schools should be concerned, for both students and teachers. All too often, however, we find that the schooling experience has just the opposite effect, and is thus actually inimical to the emergence of inquiry. As Dewey comments:

> Bacon's saying that we must become as little children in order to enter the kingdom of science is at once a reminder of the open-minded and flexible wonder of childhood and of the ease with which this endowment is lost. Some lose it in indifference or carelessness; others in a frivolous flippancy; many escape these evils only to become encased in a hard dogmatism that is equally fatal to this spirit of wonder. (Dewey, 1933, p. 39)

Indeed, it is this "spirit of wonder" that undergirds intellectual curiosity, and its loss affects all types of learning and inquiry. As Thomas Green has argued, "One way to destroy the motivation to learn is to effectively abort the childlike capacity for awe and wonder" (Green, 1971, p. 201).

Closely related to intellectual curiosity as a condition for individual inquiry is motivation. Just as educators concern themselves with motivating students in the classroom, so too must we consider the need for personal motivation in building on and responding to intellectual curiosity. Central to the idea of motivation in this regard is the need for the object of our inquiry to constitute, in Dewey's words, a "real" problem. As Dewey notes, "It is indispensable to discriminate between a genuine and simulated or mock problems . . . . Is the experience a personal thing of such a nature as inherently to stimulate and direct observation of the connections involved, and to lead to inference and its testing? Or is it imposed from without . . ."

(Dewey, 1944, p. 155). If the object or purpose of the inquiry is really a legitimate problem, in short, then the need for motivation is met; otherwise, the inquiry is simply an external (and, essentially, a nonreflective) activity that will have little benefit to the individual involved.

For true inquiry to take place, it is essential that the individual be open to differing—and even unexpected and surprising—evidence and interpretations. The teachers in every one of the five case studies presented above demonstrated such openness to the process of inquiry, although, to be sure, they pursued their inquiries in very different ways. An important element of this openness to the process of inquiry is the recognition that in any inquiry the evidence (factual data, observations, and so on) does not "speak for itself"; rather, in every instance, the observer/inquirer must make sense of the evidence by placing it in a conceptual and theoretical context. As the philosopher of science, Paul Feyerabend, has explained: "On closer analysis we even find that science knows no 'bare facts' at all but that the 'facts' that enter our knowledge are already viewed in a certain way and are, therefore, essentially ideational" (Feyerabend, 1978, p. 19). In other words, to a certain extent any organization that we impose on reality is just that—an imposition that we employ to help us understand and make sense of reality, rather than an actual picture of reality. This means that we must strive to consider and reflect upon not only the evidence that would appear to support our own construction of reality, but also (perhaps especially) evidence that does *not* fit our expectations.

Finally, an important aspect of inquiry is that we must remain open to challenge and criticism. Inquiry is best understood as a social and public endeavor and is often most effectively undertaken in a communal context. This does not necessarily mean that the actual inquiry undertaken must be a group activity, but it does mean that the process, as well as the results of the inquiry, must be subject to the scrutiny and evaluation of others. This scrutiny and evaluation can take place in many different ways: the defense of a university thesis or dissertation, the submission of the results of an inquiry to a scholarly journal, the presentation of an inquiry at a public or professional meeting, the discussion of the inquiry in informal settings with colleagues, and so on. Although it is true that none of us much

likes or enjoys being told that we are wrong, in error, or that we
have overlooked an important aspect of a context we are studying,
such corrections are essential if our inquiries are to be credible ones.

A Culture of Inquiry in the School

Thus far, we have discussed the concept of inquiry and have
indicated some of the general attributes that would characterize the
individual teacher as she or he engages in inquiry. At this point we
need to turn our focus from the individual to the school community,
and try to describe what a school in which a culture of inquiry has
been developed would look like. It is important to remember that
in any school, some inquiry will be taking place. Individual teachers,
in their daily lives, very often engage in informal types of inquiry
as part of their normal classroom activities. This chapter, for instance, began with the case of Janet Rivers, who was clearly engaged
in inquiry, though of an informal sort. Often, too, individual teachers
will seek to engage in more formal types of inquiry. While all of this
is to the good, it does not on its own mean that the school in which
these teachers work models a culture of inquiry, any more than a
school in which some teachers are bilingual would automatically be
a bilingual school. Rather, a school in which a culture of inquiry
exists is one in which there is a broad, fairly general consensus about
the desirability of and need for inquiry as part of the educational
process. In such a school, teachers, administrators, and students, as
well as university faculty where possible, will all, to varying degrees,
participate in the identification and exploration of topics of inquiry.
As the authors of the Holmes Group report *Tomorrow's Schools*
comment:

> Inquiry in the Professional Development School should be
> a way for teachers, administrators, and professors to come
> together on equal footing. It should help forge a shared profes-
> sional identity in schools and universities. And it should
> serve as a professional norm around which collaboration

can take place, bringing together the many parties who are concerned for improving schools. (Holmes Group, 1990, p. 60)

A culture of inquiry, in short, entails not merely teachers engaged in inquiry, but teachers and others collaboratively and collegially seeking better to understand and thus improve aspects of the schooling experience. For a culture of inquiry to exist and be maintained in a school requires an ongoing commitment to valuing curiosity, mutual respect, and support among teachers and between teachers and administrators; a willingness to try new ideas and practices; and finally, the ability to remain open to the unforeseen and unexpected. Further, an important element of such a school will be the nature of the leadership present, as we will discuss in detail in Chapter 4. In the Gilbert and Sullivan operetta *The Gondoliers*, the Duke of Plaza-Toro is humorously described as "leading his regiment from behind." Without dwelling on the point here, let us just note that it is simply not possible to have a school in which a culture of inquiry exists led by an administrator who exemplifies what might be termed the "Duke of Plaza-Toro" style of leadership. The school in which a culture of inquiry exists will, then, be a very unusual kind of institution, and will in many ways operate quite differently than do most schools today. It will, in short, be a school in which inquiry plays a key role in the development and process of reflective, analytic practice.

The Teacher as Researcher

An important component of a school in which a culture of inquiry exists is that teachers will see themselves, and will be seen by others, as engaging in ongoing inquiry-based activities. Such involvement in research on the part of teachers is arguably a key part of the development of reflective, analytic practice on the part of the classroom teacher. As Bogdan and Biklen explain, "Because teachers acting as researchers not only perform their duties but also watch themselves, they step back and, distanced from immediate conflicts, they are able to gain a larger view of what is happening" (Bogdan

& Biklen, 1992, p. 218). At this point, we turn to several case studies in which we can see teachers functioning as teacher-researchers.

Phonics or Whole Language?

Sara Bidwell is an experienced second grade teacher in a small elementary school in Sweetmore, a semirural area. She is the only second grade teacher in the school and, therefore, has a wide range of ability levels represented in her classroom. In recent years, Sara has also had several students with learning disabilities mainstreamed in her classroom for large portions of the day. This year, there are 20 students in Sara's class; the range of abilities is the greatest that she has experienced thus far in her career.

One of the most important parts of her job, Sara believes, is the teaching of reading. Over the years, Sara has relied on phonics and the use of basal readers as her primary method of instruction in teaching children to read. She has been very successful with about half of her students each year, with many of the children in her classes achieving at or even above grade level. At the same time, however, Sara has noticed that many other children in her classes have been considerably less successful in learning to read. In particular, she is concerned that the students are not doing as well on comprehension as she believes they can. In her early years of teaching, Sara believed that the students who were having problems learning to read were themselves to blame. Very often these children had other problems in school as well, and Sara had thought that perhaps they were just not as bright or as motivated as their more successful classmates.

During the past few years, however, Sara has changed her mind, as she has become less critical of her students and more critical of her own teaching. She has become especially concerned with the basal readers that she was once quite happy with; now she sees them as too restrictive and boring for the children she is trying to teach. Although Sara has been ready for a change of some sort for several years, she hasn't felt comfortable or sure enough to try any radical changes. Instead, she has been gradually trying to use more trade books in her teaching, and has gone out of her way to find stories and poems that she thinks her second graders will find interesting.

During the summer, the Sweetmore Board of Education, whose membership has almost completely changed as a result of the last two town elections, hired both a new superintendent and a new principal for the elementary school. For the first time in Sweetmore's history, both of these administrators are women, and both were hired by the School Board with a mandate for change. The principal of the elementary school has made it clear that one of her major goals for the current school year is to encourage teachers to vary curricula and instructional methods to suit individual student needs, interests, and learning styles. To support such changes, some funding has been made available for workshops, in-service training, university courses, curricular materials, and technical assistance. This is a significant departure from past practice in Sweetmore, and many of the teachers remain skeptical about whether the administration and school board are really serious about these changes. Sara, however, has been very excited about these efforts from the very beginning and has decided to seize the opportunity to address some of her concerns about teaching reading.

Based on several articles that she has read in her teacher magazines, Sara has decided to learn all that she can about the *whole language philosophy*. With the assistance of the new principal, she has written a professional development plan for the school year. The plan requires that she take a course at the local university that will deal with whole language, and that she will do additional professional reading in her spare time. She will also attend a workshop at the state Reading Association conference, where there will be sessions on both whole language and "Reading Recovery." A key part of Sara's professional development plan is that she will, on the basis of her classroom applications of what she learns, conduct some type of research study, which is to be completed by the end of June. Sara has already been to the university library and has selected a number of recent books concerned with whole language and the teaching of reading.

On the advice of a friend who recently graduated from a teacher preparation program, Sara has decided to keep a journal to document what takes place during the year. Her journal consists of two parts: The left side of each page is used to record ideas and information that she gets from her reading, her university course, in-service sessions, in capturing conversations she has with her colleagues, and so on; the right side of each page in her journal is used for comments to herself about the ideas and information that she is gaining. It is the left side of the journal that Sara initially thought would be the most useful, but she has since decided that it is really the comments on the right side, where she is actually reflecting, conducting ongoing dialogue with herself, trying to make sense of all that she is learning, and attempting to figure out how to apply this to her classroom, that is in truth the more valuable part of the journal.

At this point, Sara does not yet know exactly how she is going to implement the whole language philosophy in her classroom, so her plans for conducting some sort of research remain very vague. She is undecided about whether she can, or should, try to use some kind of experimental design in her research, and is aware of the fact that since she has only one class, this could be difficult (see Jaeger, 1988; Kerlinger, 1973). She is quite sure that some of the more important information about what works in her classroom will probably come from systematic observations of individual students, but she is unsure about how to make such observations. The principal has suggested trying to get students from the local university to assist her with these observations, but Sara is not sure about who to contact. She also knows that she wants to introduce student portfolios, and portfolio assessment, in her class. If she goes ahead with this, she should be able to collect quite a bit of documentary evidence about changes that are taking place with individual students. Although she isn't certain about how to do it, Sara also thinks that she probably ought to include some kind of pre- and post-test information if she wants to convince other teachers and parents, as well as other members of the community, that the changes have really had beneficial outcomes, thereby influencing subsequent policy decisions.

As she thinks about what she is trying to accomplish, and how different this school year has been from her earlier experiences, Sara is exhausted and a bit overwhelmed. She is also excited, though, and this is a feeling that makes her feel that she just may be on to something.

Understanding the Dropout Problem

Center Park High School is a large inner-city school with a total enrollment of approximately 1,800 students. The majority of the students at Center Park High School come from single-parent families, and the rate of unemployment and underemployment in the area is among the highest in the city. The crime rate has been rising dramatically in recent years, and school violence has also been increasing. Demographically, the student body is roughly 60% Hispanic, 30% African-American, 5% Asian, and 5% white. The staff at Center Park High School includes several Hispanic and African-American teachers, but nevertheless remains overwhelmingly white.

Center Park High School is fortunate in that it has many teachers and administrators who are experienced, skilled, effective, and committed to the students. Nonetheless, in spite of the staff's best efforts, nearly half the ninth grade class will drop out before 10th grade each year. This has been an ongoing problem at Center Park High School, and in the past few years, the ninth grade teachers have become more vocal about their frustrations and concerns with the situation. This year, a core group of ninth grade teachers has decided to work together to try to address this problem.

The teachers began by deciding that a big part of the problem may be the lack of information that they have about their students and the lives they lead. They agreed that they had a limited amount of factual knowledge about their students, and that while this knowledge, together with their intuition (informed as it was by their experience and concern), was useful, it was also incomplete. After reading and discussing Michelle Fine's (1991) book *Framing Dropouts*, which had been suggested to one of the teachers by the principal, the teachers decided that the best way for them to start addressing the dropout problem was by outlining the assumptions that they have been making about their students, and agreed on the following list:

1. Many parents do not care about their children's achievement in school.
2. Many students have no place to study.

3. Many students who are at risk for dropping out work long hours after school and at night to help their families financially.

4. Some students come to school not for any academic or vocational reason, but rather to socialize with other students.

5. Some of the students at risk for dropping out are already involved in the drug culture.

6. Some of the students at risk for dropping out understand and speak very little English.

7. Many of the students at risk for dropping out appear to have learned very little in elementary and middle school.

After compiling this list, the teachers formed four task groups to try to determine the extent to which their assumptions were well founded. The first task group was assigned the job of examining the cumulative records of all of the ninth graders from the previous year, in the hope of finding patterns that would help predict which types of students are most likely to drop out of school. Particular attention was paid to attendance records, grades, test scores, and teacher comments about behavior and achievement. The second task group was to try to locate students from the previous year's ninth grade who had dropped out, and to interview them about why they decided to leave school. The third task group was to try to duplicate the efforts of the second task group, but instead of interviewing dropouts, was to interview students who are now 10th graders at Center Park High School, in an effort to understand why they stayed in school. The fourth task group was assigned the job of interviewing parents of both dropouts and those students who continued on at Center Park High School to determine what the parental and extra-school contribution to this decision may have been.

When the core group of ninth grade teachers met together in January to share their findings, they were surprised to discover how much more complex and complicated the situation was than they had expected. They found that many of their assumptions had indeed proven to be true for particular students, but not, as a general rule, anywhere near the extent that they had anticipated. For instance, they found that while a few parents were uninterested in the school and their children's success or failure at school, most cared deeply about their children's successes and problems at school. They also found, much to their surprise, that for many parents the school was a hostile, alien environment, and that feelings of disempowerment on the part of parents were common when faced with school problems.

A common theme among both students who had dropped out and those who had remained in school was that the need for employment played a central role in the students' lives, and that as a result of their work roles, they often had no spare time in which to study, and further, frequently came to school too tired to pay much attention to what was taking place in class.

Many of the students who had dropped out of school reported that they had been able to coast through their earlier schooling, but had suddenly realized that they did not have the background knowledge to even begin the ninth grade curriculum. They also appeared generally to lack even fairly basic study skills that should have been learned earlier in their school experiences. As a consequence, they had not understood what was taking place in the classroom, felt stupid when comparing themselves to their more successful classmates, and could not remember enough of the material presented in class to pass the tests. Rather than have others see them as less intelligent, these students commonly chose to drop out rather than admit their problems.

The core group of teachers was especially surprised when they came to the discussion of drug use among those who dropped out. While those who had dropped out did have a much higher rate of drug abuse than those who had remained in school, in many cases this seemed to have been a consequence of having dropped out rather than the other way around.

The task group that examined the students' cumulative records was able to provide some interesting information as well. The records indicated that there was, as expected, a strong correlation between high absenteeism and subject matter failures. The task group also found, in their study of teacher comments, that in some cases a single student might be described in very different ways by different teachers. This had led the group to examine teacher grades, and they found that some teachers (including several who had reputations as "good" teachers) had had, year after year, very high rates of student failures. Since these teachers were spread throughout the school, teaching different subjects, if an at-risk student were unlucky enough to find himself or herself in classes with several of these "hard graders," the student was almost certain to fail.

Finally, in talking with both dropouts and students who had continued at Center Park High School, the teachers discovered two consistent, and powerful, themes. First, for all of the students that they talked with, the teachers discovered that there was little sense of belonging. Even though there were teachers who cared, the constant changing of subjects and teachers left little time for sustained assistance or interaction. Second, much of the curriculum was, from the students' perspective, boring and inactive, and far too much instruction consisted solely of lecture. One of the students interviewed commented in passing that learning was "when you copy down in your notebook what the teacher says."

By the end of their meeting, the core group of ninth grade teachers felt that they had a much better, albeit in many ways more complicated, view of how the students viewed school. Now they felt ready to move on and try to change things.

Using Computers to Teach Writing

Paul Roper is in his fifth year of teaching English at Dr. Martin Luther King, Jr., Middle School, which is a magnet school for mathematics, science, and technology in a medium-size city. The students at King Middle School are representative of the city's population, and include children from diverse ethnic and economic backgrounds, as well as students with a wide range of aptitudes, interests, and abilities.

Paul has found a common denominator in this diversity, however. Most of his students are poor writers. The more successful students in his classes are able to produce technically correct writing, but it is almost always forced. Many of his students, though, cannot even prepare a decent one-page essay. This has been very disturbing to Paul, who has always had his students write a great deal. Because he believes writing to be very important both academically and socially, Paul has tried to return the corrected papers to his students within a day—a practice that he definitely believes to be effective, but which has also used up much of his "non-school" time. As a result of his efforts, Paul has been a more successful writing teacher than many of his colleagues, but he is far from satisfied with his performance, since he believes that far more could be done.

Recently, Paul has stopped using textbooks altogether, and instead has been using a variety of short stories, novels, essays, and poems. This new approach seems to have created much greater student interest and has led to far more lively discussions in class, but Paul has not yet noticed any significant improvement in his students' writing. Although he is not comfortable with the technology, Paul has begun to think about using the school's computer lab as a way of encouraging students to write. He has noticed that Steve Major, a special education teacher at King Middle School, seems to have had remarkable success using the lab; some of his students, who had never written much of anything before, are now writing three to four pages. In addition, the students' interactions with the computer seem to have made them more willing to rewrite their papers, as well as more animated and willing to share and discuss their work with others. Steve believes that his students have really "found their voice" for the first time, writing about personal issues in their lives, and has strongly recommended that Paul give the computer lab a try.

Paul is interested in trying the lab, but would like to do so in an experimental way. He has two classes of seventh graders that are quite similar, with roughly comparable levels of writing ability. His goal is to use the lab with one group, and his other methods with the other class, and to then compare the results. He is very much unsure, though, of what exactly to do, and is afraid that his inexperience in both using the computer lab and conducting research will prevent him from accomplishing anything worthwhile. Paul begins to think about the different ways he could organize the instruction for each class and then assess the difference in outcomes. He wonders how many factors he should keep the same and how many he could change at one time and still be able to determine what made a difference and what didn't. Could he use an experimental or quasi-experimental design? Should he use pre- and post-tests to assess gains, and if so, what tests would fit with the curriculum? Research methods of this type would give strength to his conclusions, no matter what the outcome might be. But would he really gain deeper understanding and insights into what had taken place?

Analysis and Discussion. These three case studies provide us with a wide variety of very different kinds of school-based research scenarios. Each case presents us with both a different type of research problem and a different context in which the problem is to be addressed. Further, two of the cases (Sara Bidwell's concern with teaching reading and Paul Roper's concern with teaching writing) involve primarily one teacher, while the third case (Center Park High School and its dropout problem) is a collaborative effort involving a number of teachers. All three of these cases, however, exemplify the concern raised earlier in this chapter about the need for developing a culture of inquiry in the school, and all three cases are, ultimately, concerned with what might be called action research in the school setting (see Bissex & Bullock, 1987; Goswami & Stillman, 1987; Kemmis & McTaggart, 1988).

The three cases are similar in another important way as well. In all three cases, the research problem is the result of a concern or question raised by teachers on the basis of their own observations and experiences in the classroom and school context. That is, the research questions that these teachers are trying to address arise from their own curiosity and worries, and not as a result of a literature search of some sort. This is an important point because it is one of the ways in which action research tends to differ from more traditional kinds of educational research. In other words, in all three of these case studies we see examples of what might be called *teacher-driven* research.

These three case studies are also useful for us because they provide an array of possibilities with respect to appropriate research methodologies. One lesson that should be clear from these cases is that there is no single method of research that could answer all of the different questions that have been raised; indeed, what these three cases would lead us to believe is that there is no single model of inquiry, and that research is best viewed as a dynamic, rather than a static, process that seeks to take into account the incredible complexity of human beings and human social settings (such as classrooms). The task of the professional educator must be to examine the research question she or he is faced with and make a determination about which of the myriad possible research methodologies will be best suited to providing the kind of information desired There is no more a "correct" approach to research than there is a "correct" way of teaching a child to read; different approaches and methodologies must be used in each case, and the determination of which approach and method should be tried in any particular context is the responsibility of the teacher as an educational professional. At this point, let us examine each of the three case studies and try to identify the kinds of research methodologies that might be most appropriate in each case.

In the case of Sara Bidwell, we have a classroom teacher who has been monitoring what works, and what doesn't work, in her own classroom as she tries to teach children to read. For Sara, the impetus for inquiry is not an abstract curiosity, nor is it a puzzle that has emerged in the professional literature. Rather, it is the kind of concern that almost all classroom teachers face as a result of their daily classroom practice. Sara has begun with her problem—how to do a better job teaching children in her class to read—and has also committed herself to learning more about alternative approaches to the teaching of reading with which she is not yet really familiar. She has, in short, already made an effort to link the topic and focus of her personal inquiry to the existing professional knowledge base. Further, Sara has taken the critical step of deciding, at least in tentative form, how she is going to go about addressing her inquiry. By using a split-page journal, Sara has ensured that she will be able to track her own growing database as well as her own understanding of that database. In essence, keeping a reflective journal provides a simple and integrated method of combining conversations, observations, insights, and so on as we construct our understanding of what is taking place. The format of the journal also allows us the luxury of backtracking and watching our own process of discovery and understanding. It is through such systematic means that teachers can review and challenge their own thinking, understandings, and practice, and, ultimately, can help contribute to the knowledge base in their own profession. This is one of the ways in which truly dedicated professionals can be distinguished from other workers.

Sara's process of inquiry hinges on the changes that she will be implementing in her classroom, and it is really not possible for her to decide what sort of study she wishes to conduct until she has decided what exactly she is going to do in terms of implementing the whole language philosophy in her classroom, and what her goals for these changes are. Once she has come up with a plan for implementing the change in her teaching, there is a wide array of possible research methods she could employ. She has already decided that she would like to include in her study some sort of pre- and post-test, presumably of reading ability, comprehension, and so forth. Such pre- and post-testing can be combined with other types of research activities as well, including individual case studies of students, comparisons of the reading achievement of Sara's students with comparable students receiving a more traditional kind of instruction, and so on. It would also be possible for Sara to focus her study not so much on improvement in student learning, but on changes in students' attitudes about reading. Obviously, one would go about studying such attitudinal changes in a somewhat different manner than if improvements in reading comprehension, for example, were the focus of one's research. In short, what Sara's experience makes clear is that it is important to decide what kinds of things one wants to know before specific research strategies can be adopted and implemented.

In the case of Center Park High School, we are presented with collaborative research being undertaken by a group of ninth grade teachers, who share a concern about the problem of the ninth grade dropout rate at their school. Again, as was the case with Sara Bidwell, these teachers have identified a problem in their own experience to study. Although the problem they are trying to address is a common one in urban schools, one about which there has been extensive discussion in the professional literature, the teachers themselves are interested in the problem primarily because it affects them and their students. Although no mention is made in this case of anyone keeping a journal, the teachers together engage in a process that is very similar in purpose to at least some aspects of a reflective journal. Specifically, the teachers begin by making a list of the things that they believe to be true that relate to the high dropout rate. In essence, this means they are engaging in both individual and group reflection. Once they have completed their list of assumptions, they then use that list as the basis for their inquiry. Based on the beliefs that they identified as their starting assumptions (their hypotheses, to use research jargon), they divide themselves into four task groups and try to determine the extent to which each of their assumptions is valid. Each of the task groups makes use of somewhat different strategies, determined in large part by the kind of information they are seeking. For instance, the first task group, which focused on the analysis of student cumulative records, would have utilized basic statistical procedures to identify correlations among such variables as attendance, grades, test scores, teacher comments, and the likelihood of an individual student's dropping out of school. The other three task groups all made use of interviewing techniques. This combination of quantitative and qualitative research methods helps to ensure that the information the teachers gather will provide as complete a picture as possible of what is taking place. An important aspect of the Center Park High School collaborative study is that the teachers remained open to surprises; they were willing to see their starting assumptions proven wrong, or at least misleading. This openness to being wrong is arguably the most important element, not only of any sort of research activity but also of reflection and reflective practice. Finally, it is worth noting that the only outcome of the Center Park High School study thus far is a greater understanding of what is taking place on the part of the teachers; the next step, which is not detailed in our case study, is for the teachers to attempt to fashion a response to their new understanding of the problem.

Paul Roper presents an interesting case because he exemplifies the Deweyan notion of problem solving that we have already discussed (see Dewey, 1910, 1933, 1938). He is puzzled by his students' lack of writing skills and is intrigued by the potential he believes may exist in the use of computers. His approach is basically an openminded one; it isn't at all clear that he is sure the use of computers with his students will be as successful as it has been for Steve Major, but he is willing to try. He is deliberating seeking a research methodology that will allow him to compare two comparable groups, and is cognizant of the fact that his own inexperience in using computers may be a factor. In short, he has already decided, in a tentative fashion, on the appropriate research design for his study, as well as on some of the limitations of that study.

What holds all three of these cases together is the curiosity of the teacher-researcher as the original motivating force for the research endeavor. A closely related aspect of this common theme is that in all three cases the teacher or group of teachers see themselves as the primary researchers; they may make use of other resources, but they maintain their ownership of the study. This emphasis on ownership, in fact, is arguably the most significant way in which teacher-based action research differs from other, more traditional research. As Bogdan and Biklen have noted,

> Research is a frame of mind—a perspective people take toward objects and activities. Academicians and professional researchers investigate questions that are of interest to them. They state the purpose of their study in the form of hypotheses or research questions. They are not only expected to conduct research, but are urged to do so along the lines of established research traditions, whether quantitative or qualitative. While colleagues argue, they share a consensus about what it means to do research. Outside the academy, people in the "real world" also can conduct research—research that is practical, directed at their own concerns and, for those who wish, a tool to bring about social change. (Bogdan & Biklen, 1992, p. 223)

Classroom teachers are presented with a wide range of possible research topics every day in their classrooms; many of these topics are significant and important to the teachers' effectiveness in the classroom (see Kemmis & McTaggart, 1988; Mohr & MacLean, 1987). An important part of becoming a reflective practitioner is the ability to recognize these topics and to seek, in whatever manner seems most appropriate, to resolve them.

Propositions for Reflection and Consideration

1. There is no single model of inquiry that includes all cases and types of educational inquiry. Inquiry can be more or less

formal, more or less rigorous; can involve a wide range of different techniques and methods; and can even entail very different (and sometimes incompatible) ideas and assumptions about the nature of knowledge and knowing.

2. Inquiry is a dynamic rather than a static process, and always takes place in a social and cultural context.

3. The individual characteristics necessary for inquiry to take place are intellectual curiosity, motivation, openness in inquiry, and openness to challenge.

4. Classroom-based inquiry should begin with a problem or puzzle that is of real concern and interest to the teacher, to ensure that the teacher has ownership of the research study.

5. A school that exemplifies a culture of inquiry entails not merely teachers engaged in inquiry, but teachers and others collaboratively and collegially seeking to better understand and thus improve aspects of the schooling experience. This requires an ongoing commitment to valuing curiosity, mutual respect, and support among teachers and between teachers and administrators; a willingness to try new ideas and practices; and finally, the ability to remain open to the unforeseen and unexpected.

Transformational Curricula
and Instruction

The traditional craft of the teacher can be rescued and strengthened by understanding the connection between the content area of the curriculum and how it will be understood by the student. Understanding this connection involves recognizing the cultural pattern of thought (the episteme*) that underlies the organization of knowledge in the curriculum unit as well as the phenomenological world of the student. The latter is essential for grasping what the student is likely to understand and how that understanding will be integrated into the student's pattern of thinking.*

C. A. Bowers (1984, p. 78)

Toward Transformational Curricula and Instruction:
Three Case Studies

Trying an Integrated Curriculum

Jack Williams is an English teacher, and Rita Lopez is a social studies teacher. Both are concerned about the 10th graders with whom they work, particularly about how many of their students will return in the fall. It is almost the end of the year, and many of the students are obviously discouraged and alienated by school.

Claremont High School, where Jack and Rita teach, is a school of about 1,100 students, racially and linguistically mixed, with many students coming from families in which unemployment and underemployment are major problems. Many of the students are not performing at grade level, as is clearly seen in the results of the state mastery test scores. The students are discouraged by a variety of factors, including not only school-based issues, but also their economic circumstances and the economic circumstances of those around them. Although they have been told repeatedly about the value of education, they don't actually see much difference in outcome between those who drop out of school and those who stay. Many of the African-American and Hispanic students believe that their skin color and language will bar them from any significant advances no matter what they do. There have been clashes between some of the different groups in the high school, a few of which have been serious. Many of the teachers at Claremont see the students as hostile, belligerent, and arrogant. Many of the students were labeled long ago as "learning disabled" or "behaviorally disordered," and these labels have continued to impact on their treatment in the school.

In recent years, Claremont has been divided into four "houses," each with its own vice-principal. The motivation for dividing the school this way was that the smaller groups would provide more of a sense of family, and that the vice-principal could get to know more students on an individual basis. To a minor degree, some of these things have occurred, but there have been no significant effects on the students' academic achievement as a consequence of the establishment of the smaller "houses" in the school.

During the current school year, there has been a faculty committee at Claremont engaged in studying different possibilities for developing some kind of thematically structured curriculum. Some of the themes that were discussed included the environment, global education, and multiculturalism. In their discussions, the teachers also considered interdisciplinary team-teaching approaches, as well as alternative scheduling possibilities that would allow a team of teachers to work with the same small group of students, in different subjects, for most of the day. They had initially been enthusiastic about trying such a thematic approach that would allow more in-depth and integrated treatment of topics that would be of interest and concern to their students.

During one of the spring faculty meetings, the committee reported back on its work to the entire faculty. The reaction to the committee's report and suggestions was swift and angry. Some teachers took the position that, "these kids can't handle that kind of curriculum complexity." Others argued that the students needed tight structures and strong discipline to keep them under control. Several teachers asserted that an integrated curriculum would inevitably water down everything, and in any event simply pandered to students' interests. As one teacher commented, "These kids barely can say their name and maybe write it, and you want them to tackle these kinds of topics? Get real." One teacher made an eloquent speech on the necessity of good lectures and note-taking skills as real education; he went on to note this was essential for those few that will go on to real colleges, and for the rest, it would be beneficial for them to learn how to pay attention. The committee's suggestions were rejected, and no follow-up was proposed.

Jack and Rita, who had both been involved in the proposal, felt hurt and defeated. A few days after the meeting, Rita suggested to Jack that they try some of the ideas the committee had recommended, on a much smaller scale, with one class of 11th graders they might share the next year. They spoke with the principal, and she agreed to schedule a group of students in back-to-back classes each day, and also to schedule Jack and Rita for alternating free periods so that both could be involved with the same group for an hour and a half each day, though it would also mean that both teachers gave up their one free period.

This arrangement meant that they could integrate the curriculum around themes that were relevant to the lives of their students. Both Rita and Jack believed that they would be able to draw on a wide variety of sources from social studies and literature.

The methodology that Jack and Rita have agreed upon involves their selecting a major theme and presenting it in a question form to the class, then having the students identify the smaller questions embedded inside the larger question. Readings from newspapers, journals, technical reports, short stories, essays, novels, poetry, plays, films, and various historical documents will be used rather than the regular textbooks. Different students will accept responsibility for reading and reporting back to the class about various documents. Subgroups will decide on other ways to explore the theme as well. For example, one group might decide to interview a variety of people in the community around a set of questions they put together, based on their reading, discussions, and interests. Depending on the theme, some students might decide to videotape certain kinds of situations in the community, while others might search out various kinds of records relevant to their investigation at the courthouse and in local libraries. Others would find pertinent information in museums of various types.

Rita and Jack agree that they will give the students room to explore a variety of avenues within each theme. The instructional "glue" that will hold the classes together will be the frequent group sessions in which individuals and small groups share what they have collected about the topic, what they think it means, and where it leads them next. Jack and Rita agree that they will require frequent short reports summarizing the same information, to ensure that the students are developing a number of different skills at the same time. During the course of the year, students will be encouraged both to work in small groups and to do some work on their own. All of the students will be expected to keep a daily journal, both to allow Rita and Jack to monitor their progress and to identify possible problems. The students will also be encouraged to use their journals to share personal feelings and reflections on their lives with Jack and Rita.

Although they know they have a great deal of planning ahead of them, Rita and Jack are excited about next year, and wish that they could figure out a way to have the same group for longer than their hour and a half.

Toward an Environmental Curriculum

Yorkshire Middle School is in an upper class district near a major U.S. city; it is the quintessential bedroom community for the upper and near-upper levels of corporate America. Many of the well-to-do families in the area send their children to private schools. While the parents of these students are not publicly active in community politics and institutions, they nevertheless wield much influence on community decisions behind the scenes, most often in the interest of keeping the local tax rates "reasonable."

When visiting schools in the district for the first time, one is struck by how much the school buildings look like those in poorer areas of the city. Repainting is sorely needed, custodial services are at a minimum, and instructional equipment is only slightly better than that seen elsewhere in the area. On the other hand, when talking with the teachers at Yorkshire, it quickly becomes clear that there is an impressive number of very capable and creative teachers here. Nonetheless, these teachers, like all other public school teachers, are confined by state and district demands and constraints; in fact, in some ways they are *more* constrained because of the high, and narrow, expectations that parents in such districts have. The pressures are enormous and often stultifying. Thus, although the curricula at Yorkshire, and in many similar schools, may appear to be more advanced because the reading sources and course titles are more sophisticated and the teachers are often (though by no means always) better educated than their counterparts in other systems, nevertheless one commonly finds that the students in schools such as Yorkshire appear to be as bored and disengaged as students in any other district. This is the reality of Yorkshire and many other districts nationwide that are often cited as beacons for other schools. Do not such claims, at root, suggest that we should take credit for genetics or assume that wealth guarantees academic achievement? What is the "boredom factor"?

Anne Jacobs and Maura Quinn have worked together at Yorkshire Middle School for the past 10 years. Students always seem more engaged in their classes than they do in many others. Anne is a science teacher and Maura is an English teacher. Anne is very involved in environmental issues, both locally and regionally, while Maura has been active in the human rights movement. They have both been active members in a number of regional environmental groups and share a love of nature.

Anne and Maura are also very suspect in the community, primarily because they have both visibly challenged local and state environmental policies, as well as the effects of the consumer-oriented life-style prevalent in Yorkshire County. Many parents have also voiced concerns about the two teachers, although no one has challenged the very real success that Anne and Maura have had with their students.

Anne and Maura have decided that they want to integrate the entire science and English curricula for grade eight around the general theme of "nature writing." Grade eight is a review year for all subjects and, therefore, is often especially boring for most students. Anne and Maura believe that by teaching science and English around the theme of "nature writing," they will be able to utilize their own vocational and avocational expertise and interests, while at the same time capturing a natural interest of students at that age. Such an approach will also provide their students with an opportunity to synthesize their skills and knowledge by using them in a creative, practical fashion. As an added benefit, the students will confront their relationship with the natural world, and will be asked to relate that relationship with global politics. Although Anne and Maura know that this may cause some students, and perhaps some parents, a degree of discomfort, they nonetheless believe that the activity will be valuable and worthwhile, and that it is clearly educationally desirable.

Anne and Maura decide they will begin with selected works from three naturalists representing different historical periods: Emerson, Teale, and Dillard. Each writer represents a different and distinct connection with the natural world, and all are superb writers. The teachers believe that these three writers are also a good choice because they present very different natural history interests, while at the same time demonstrating the universality and timelessness of many environmental issues.

After devoting considerable time and energy to planning how they would accomplish this integration, Anne and Maura present their concept and plans to the principal at Yorkshire Middle School. The principal indicates that he has some reservations, but agrees to allow the teachers to present their proposal to the board of education. At the next meeting of the board, Ann and Maura present their plans, and are met with considerable hostility and rejection. Some members of the board reacted with concerns about how the content that Anne and Maura propose to teach will relate to the questions on the S.A.T. examination, while others expressed concern that this sort of exploration might lead to negative views about business and politicians. One member of the board questioned the motives of the two teachers, who, she argued, were known to be active participants in "left-wing environmental groups." This board member also commented, as an aside, that, "isn't strange that these two single women not only spend all their non-work time together but now want to teach together as well?"

Refocusing the Curriculum on the Community

Redford School is located in northern New England near the Canadian border. It is a community of about 2,200 people, including both townspeople and those living in the nearby countryside. The nearest sizable population center is a declining mill town of about 5,000 people. The population in Redford is fairly evenly divided between those of French-Canadian heritage and those of old Yankee lineage. The French-Canadians are mostly bilingual, except for a tiny number of elderly citizens, while the Yankees are almost entirely monolingual.

The school is a single building, with separate corridors for the K-8 and 9-12 students. Altogether, there are some 450 students at Redford School: 325 in grades K-8, and 125 in grades 9-12. The dropout rate is around 25%. Of the high school graduates, only 20% go to college. Very few of the students at Redford are likely to leave the area for employment elsewhere. Most people in the area do a variety of things to earn a living; nearly everyone does small-scale farming, at least enough to supply one's family and trade with neighbors. In addition, depending on one's skills, people do a variety of odd jobs, either for pay or to barter for other products or skills. Summer tourists are a major source of income. The tourists are not wealthy people coming to resorts, but rather families coming to lake cottages, but they still provide a number of small economic opportunities for many people. The population of Redford is proud and literate, and for the most part doesn't complain about life circumstances.

The curriculum of the school is fairly standard by state guidelines, but cannot afford vocational education programs, art, or music. The classes are about average size. The teachers, while fairly conservative in terms of teaching style and discipline, are clearly caring. Further, the teachers at Redford School are almost all from the area; this is a town where everyone knows everyone, and families and friendships go back for years and years.

Denise Goddu is the third grade teacher at Redford. She was born, raised, and went to school in the town. She went to college at the state university, majoring in history and elementary education —a combined major that took her 5 years to complete. She then went to teach in a suburban district of a nearby state for 5 years. Last year, she returned to teach in Redford.

Rob Williams is the fourth grade teacher and has been teaching in Redford for 10 years. This has been his only teaching job since college. Rob was born and raised in another state, in an urban area, and had actively sought a different life-style, which he found in Redford.

Denise and Rob are both dedicated teachers who want learning to be more exciting and successful for their students. As they look at the curriculum and instruction in the first and second grade, and at their own instruction, they are concerned that there is too much reliance on rote learning and sequential learning, as well as workbooks and ditto sheets. Students are generally all doing the same thing at the same time. There seems to be a lack of excitement in the students. Denise and Rob are also concerned that most instruction and curriculum materials are in English, even though many of their French-Canadian students are clearly struggling with the language. Most of all, they realize that they and their colleagues are not teaching the students how to construct and implement their own learning; rather, the entire schooling experience consists of dependent learning. At the same time, Denise and Rob are very much aware that the parents are satisfied with the school because it is the same as it was when they were in the school.

Denise and Rob decide they want to combine their two classes for 3 weeks and teach an integrated unit that would explore local history, but in the process would also involve language arts, science, math, art, and some basic French. The unit will involve work outside of school on a number of days as well. After lengthy discussions with the principal, and a meeting with the superintendent, they receive permission to proceed. First, they must get signed permissions from the parents because of the out-of-school experiences. Rather than just sending notes home, Denise and Rob decide to hold an evening meeting to explain what they intend to do and why they think the experience will be a worthwhile one for the students. The meeting is well attended. Many questions are asked, and while the parents are skeptical, they like and trust these teachers and agree to give the 3-week experiment a try.

Denise and Rob then spend a morning with their two classes together in the school auditorium, explaining in general terms what they plan to do. The students have many of the same concerns that their parents had—after all, what was being suggested was different from anything they were familiar with. However, the lure of not having to be in the school building all the time was overpowering, and by the end of the morning, the children were as excited about the new experiment as their teachers.

The unit begins with gravestone rubbings in the oldest of the four local cemeteries. Denise and Rob give the students the necessary materials and instructions, telling them to look at a number of markers until they find one of particular interest. Each student is to do two rubbings of the same marker so they can hang one in the classroom and use the other as a reference for the next phase of the project.

Back in the classroom, the students discuss their rubbings. They talked about what could be learned from the gravestones: how long people lived, family relationships, how many generations of the same family are present, and so on. One of the children in Denise's class points out that none of the names in that graveyard is of French derivation; this leads to a long discussion of why this is so. At the suggestion of Denise's class, the children make a second outing to another old graveyard, where almost all the names are French. This, in turn, results in an extended discussion about religious differences, ethnic differences, and feelings of "separateness."

The students also discover that there is a 3-year period in the early 1700s when many people, of all ages, died. This leads some of the children to the public library to search out local history books. The children discover that during the 3-year period there had been a smallpox epidemic. This led to reading and discussions with the local doctor about how there were no medicines to fight disease and infection at that time. The students related this information to the high number of birth deaths they had discovered in their rubbings and in the courthouse records.

The students also learned that their region was once a booming area for lumbering and the making of paper. This leads them to research on how these industries were conducted during earlier times; they soon realized work then was much harder and more dangerous. The students wonder why these industries are no longer in their area. They learn what chemicals were used to form wood into paper and to bleach the paper. They discover that many workers were injured or killed during logging and manufacturing. Soon they discover that many of the people who worked in the paper mills seemed not to live as long as other people.

During the 3 weeks of the experiment, Denise and Bob's students wrote about their discoveries and observations each day. Some did paintings and drawings to represent important ideas; others took photographs. Some students became investigative reporters regarding safety protection for workers; others tried to find out where the paper industry had gone. Some wrote short stories and poems. One group decided to test the waters of the local river, streams, and ponds. All the students worked to find out where their families had come from and when they had arrived in Redford. The classes discussed the similarities and differences between French-Canadians and Yankees, and Protestant and Catholics. They wondered why there were no people of other races and religions in the town.

Finally, the students and their teachers put on an exhibit in the school auditorium for the whole school and the community, showing their artwork, photography, stories, poems, science experiments, and investigative reports, topped off with a play written and produced by the students that depicted life in earlier times. The students passed out a newspaper they had written and produced that represented one day in the 1700s in their community; it was in a two column design—one side in French and the other in English.

Analysis and Discussion. The three case studies presented above all demonstrate the potential for curricular innovation and change, but also remind us of the risks that such change can pose for the classroom teacher. These three case studies represent three levels of schooling and three quite different community settings. Very often, educators and members of the public erroneously assume that new approaches to curriculum and instruction are best limited to well-behaved, high-ability students—a view that was seen in the comments of some of the teachers at Claremont High School. Another common barrier to curricular and instructional innovation are concerns about the impact of a new approach on college-bound students, especially with respect to S.A.T. and A.C.T. scores. Concerns of this type were seen in both the Claremont and Yorkshire Middle School cases. These two barriers are common blocks to changes in curriculum and instruction, as, unfortunately, are inappropriate personal innuendoes of the kind faced by Anne and Maura.

In spite of the differences in levels of schooling and the differences in community in the three cases presented here, there are a number of common characteristics in the innovations proposed by the teachers. In all three examples, the proposed curriculum is organized around themes and takes an interdisciplinary approach combining at least two subject matter areas. Thematic approaches of these kinds provide the opportunity for students to be more active learners and experience a wider variety of learning strategies than would otherwise be likely to occur. They also give students more freedom to make determinations about what and how they learn, as well as how they will demonstrate what they have learned. Built into such an approach will be chances for students to work alone, in pairs, or in small groups at various times, as well as all together in a more traditional classroom atmosphere. This allows for a balance between individual achievement and group accomplishment. Further, using such an approach means that assignments and activities can be geared to an individual student's current level of ability, interests, and so on.

Another valuable lesson found in all three of these cases is how the teachers abandoned the narrow confines of textbooks, moving instead to a variety of primary sources, including original works, records, documents, and so forth. All of the teachers seem to have understood that textbooks are only one possible source of information for students, and are in fact arguably far from the best source if our goal is truly to engage students in the construction of their own learning. To do this, we need to learn to trust students to learn on their own, as well as in our presence. This, no doubt, will be a difficult lesson for many of us, but it is nevertheless an essential one.

A critical issue that is often discussed, but seldom implemented in meaningful ways in the schools, is the need for students to engage their learning on matters of values and problems they confront in their lives and community. In other words, students must take ownership of what they are learning—they must be empowered as learners. The challenge for us as educators, as Dewey expressed it in *The Child and the Curriculum*, is to avoid the temptation to view the subject matter as something unrelated to the child:

> Abandon the notion of subject-matter as something fixed and ready-made in itself, outside the child's experience; cease thinking of the child's experience as also something hard and fast; see it as something fluent, embryonic, vital; and we realize that the child and the curriculum are simply two limits which define a single process. Just as two points define a straight line, so the present standpoint of the child and the facts and truths of studies define instruction. It is continuous reconstruction, moving from the child's present experience out into that represented by the organized bodies of truth that we call studies. (Dewey, 1943, p. 11)

All too often adults view learning as the result of formal, direct instruction. As one child commented, in explaining why time at a camp wasn't "learning": "We don't learn anything here. Learning is when they write stuff on the board and you copy it down. We don't copy nothing down here—there aren't even chalkboards."

Although direct instruction certainly has its place in the classroom, there are many other ways in which students can learn, some of them far more appropriate for specific topics than would be traditional methods of instruction. Certainly we know that if we wish to change attitudes and behaviors, direct instruction is likely to be ineffective. Students must be given mature opportunities for engagement in social problem areas, such as AIDS, drugs, violence, abuse, environmental problems, divorce, nuclear concerns, the homeless, prejudice, gender, suicide, stress, death, sex, and many other topics that are often avoided or inadequately handled in more traditional approaches to teaching and learning. Textbooks and lectures simply do not engage students, nor do students have any sense of ownership or interest when topics are presented in this manner. Rather, they must be given opportunities for critical thinking, discussion, exploration, and presentation. For teachers to make such opportunities possible for our students will inevitably make many adults, both in and out of school, very uncomfortable and defensive—as was seen in two of our three case studies. Nevertheless, such value issues are at the heart of growing up, and dealing with them in a public and critical manner is the essence of a democracy. As Robertson has argued:

> Concerns about the vitality of American political life, citizen apathy, growing disparities among citizens in wealth and power and conflict among racial and ethnic groups make Dewey's conception of public life attractive. Communities in which all share in the creation and enjoyment of common goods, in which each person's flourishing is thought necessary for the full flourishing of the others and the individuality of each is respected, and in which conflicts are brought out in the open and resolved through public discourse surely are worthy goals. (Robertson, 1992, p. 374)

As Dewey and others have urged, the community should have a major role in curriculum and instruction, and in each of the three cases presented here, the teachers have engaged the community— sometimes successfully, sometimes (thus far, at least) not.

Toward Transformational Curricula and Instruction

Many curriculum theorists and researchers have consistently noted the discrepancy between the planned curriculum, the enacted curriculum, and the experienced curriculum (see, for example, Gehrke, Knapp, & Sirotnik, 1992). The *planned curriculum* is that presented by state and local policies and curriculum guides, often constructed by committees in absentia and usually devoid of local context, except for historical events. Many actually assume this is what is taught. The planned curriculum is reinforced by standardized or state-produced mastery tests to ensure that teachers teach what they are supposed to teach. Further buttressing is accomplished through textbook series and workbooks. This structure is premised on the belief that curriculum is, at heart, mostly discrete skills and factual knowledge, and that teachers can convey this efficiently to groups of students at the same time in the roughly the same way. Individuality, values, beliefs, and critical thinking are matters for rhetoric, but not to be practiced; instead, compliance and complacency rule. As Herbert Thelen wrote more than 30 years ago:

> It is in the formulation of the problem that individuality is expressed, that creativity is stimulated, and that nuances and subtleties are discovered. It is these aspects of inquiry that give birth to new social movements and political orientations, and that are central in the emergence of insight. Yet it is precisely these aspects of inquiry that schools ignore, for they collapse inquiry to mere problem-solving, and they keep the student busy finding "solutions" to "problems" that are already formulated, externalized, depersonalized, and emotionally fumigated. The school is concerned with the student who formulates his own problems only when he is so creative with school property that he perforce enters a "counseling" relationship (on pain of dismissal). But as far as the academic work of the school goes, personal stirrings and strivings and self-discoveries have no place. In effect, what is missing is the investment of learning with personal emotion and meaning. (Quoted in Eisner, 1982, p. 8)

Often, other nations are seen as being more successful in their schools because their students seem to succeed better on standardized tests that measure factual knowledge. John Dewey, George Counts, and many other educators have questioned whether such an approach is viable and defensible in a democratic society such as our own, and such concerns are, we would suggest, well heeded.

The *enacted curriculum* is what really happens in the classroom. This usually consists of a mixture of some of the planned curriculum, teacher additions or subtractions, teacher personality and interests, and student interests and abilities. Even though the planned curriculum and materials are often intended to be as "teacher-proof" as possible, this intention is (fortunately, we would argue) rarely realized. Too little time and effort in the planned curriculum are directed to conceptual understanding, problem solving, and critical thinking. The reliance on curriculum materials divorces what is presented in the classroom from the day-to-day realities, fears, and hopes of the student.

This brings us to the *experienced curriculum*, which is usually divorced from the lives of students and from the context in which they live. What students experience is a self-contained reality; that is, what happens in the classroom all too often has no relationship to anything else in the lives of the students. For many teachers, of course, the same is true, even though there is no direct relationship between their reality and the reality of the students. In Jerzy Kosinski's novel *Being There* (1980), as one of the characters is being mugged, his response is to keep clicking his remote control. One is tempted to ask whether much of what happens in schools is comparable to this meaningless and ineffectual clicking of the remote control. Why do we continue to persist in dehumanizing, alienating, and often meaningless practices, when in fact we know better?

Traditional approaches to curriculum are mostly tied to subject matter divisions; most curriculum development occurs within these confines. This is convenient when the primary focus is on discrete skills and factual knowledge. It is even more efficient if we track students according to ability, as in fact we do. Further, as a consequence of long-held beliefs and practices related to ideas about teaching and learning, curriculum development often focuses on relatively narrow goals and objectives, particularly those that are easily measured. This means that curricular goals must be small and simple, not large and complex. Content within the confines of subject matter becomes the prime activity—what "pieces" of knowledge should be taught/learned, in what sequence, to what depth, and with how much breadth? How should this content be organized? Such are often the guiding questions that underlie curriculum development in the schools.

Most schools also opt to avoid conflict and controversy in curriculum materials and classroom topics. Although perhaps understandable from a pragmatic and political perspective, the result of avoiding controversial topics often leads to bland and banal course topics and materials, and can hardly be seen as supportive of the development of independent and critical thinkers.

Instruction, in short, should not be separated from curriculum; the teaching method, the learning activities, the materials, and the individual interests, abilities, goals, and learning styles of the student are all part of the curriculum—no one of these should be separated from the other components.

At the beginning of this century, John Dewey sought to address what he believed to be the dualism of the relationship of the school and the society. As he wrote in *Moral Principles in Education,*

> The school cannot be a preparation for social life excepting as it reproduces, within itself, typical conditions of social life. . . . The only way to prepare for social life is to engage in social life. To form habits of social usefulness and serviceableness, apart from any direct social need and motive, apart from any existing social situation, is, to the letter, teaching the child to swim by going through motions outside of the water. The most indispensable condition is left out of account, and the results are correspondingly partial. (Dewey, 1975, p. 14)

Such a conception of learning, as well as of the relationship between the school and the community, provides a template for the creation of effective, efficient, and democratic schools. Dewey saw that children were naturally curious and had questions about the world around them—and that their own world was rich with materials and experiences that could be organized in interesting ways to pull them toward the wonders of learning. Children could learn that they had the ability to interact and have impact on the world. This engagement would produce citizens who were responsible and did not see themselves as powerless: citizens who would not be content to accept the world as it was. Reflection and inquiry, Dewey believed, were essential for all citizens in a democratic society, and it was the job of the school to promote such reflection and inquiry.

Unfortunately, nearly a century later, our schools still seem far from this ideal.

Propositions for Reflection and Consideration

1. The development of innovative, transformational curricular and instructional approaches in the classroom is an essential component of reflective practice.
2. Thematic approaches to curricular content are often common elements of innovative curricular efforts, as are approaches that seek to integrate different subject matter areas.
3. In developing transformational curricula, it is essential that teachers go beyond traditional teaching methods and materials. Textbooks, for instance, should at best be seen as points of departure for the curriculum, rather than as curricular guides themselves.
4. The distinction between curriculum and instruction is at best misleading; there is a symbiotic relationship between them that the teacher must take into account.
5. There will often be considerable resistance, from colleagues, administrators, parents, and students, to the development of novel and innovative curricular and instructional approaches. Such resistance can take a variety of forms, including academic arguments, arguments about student abilities, political challenges, and personal attacks.

Transformational Leadership
in the School

The relations of most leaders is transactional—leaders approach followers with an eye to exchanging one thing for another: jobs for votes. . . . Transforming leadership, while more complex, is more potent. The transforming leader recognizes and exploits an existing need or demand of a potential follower. But beyond that, the transforming leader looks for potential motives in followers, seeks to satisfy higher needs, and engages the full person of the follower. The result of transforming leadership is a relationship of mutual stimulation and evaluation that converts followers into leaders and may convert leaders into moral agents.

James MacGregor Burns (1979)

The Organizational Context of Leadership:
Two Case Studies

The Case of John Dewey Junior High School

John Dewey Junior High School has a student body of 1,000. Once the city's premier high school, it is located in a lower- to middle-class, urban neighborhood. Upon entering the school, we are immersed in activity in the halls as students pass to their next class—students joshing one another loudly, boys and girls talking animatedly in groups, couples holding hands, and one or two couples embracing next to their open lockers. A buzzer sounds. Students race to their next class. We ask one student for directions to the principal's office. She takes time to lead us to the office, where we are welcomed by the secretary and school principal who are working on an attendance report. The principal asks the secretary to bring us coffee. We are told that we may move freely around the school, visit any classroom we wish, and talk with any of the students, teachers, or staff. Great pride is expressed by the principal in the amount of autonomy that faculty have in developing their unique approaches to teaching. He informs us that at the last faculty meeting the staff discussed our visit and decided that we should be part of a typical school day at Dewey Junior High School. No special plans have been made. The principal tells us that staff morale is high and the faculty relates well with one another. We are given a class schedule and a floor plan of classrooms, and we become part of John Dewey Junior High School for a day.

Not only do teachers relate well with one another, but they also relate well with the students. The students are relatively uninhibited and unencumbered with social protocol. They converse easily, not only with each other but also with their teachers, even during formal lectures. Several even seek us out to discuss how they feel about being students at Dewey. Teachers maintain friendly relations with their students, creating a very informal climate. Even though behavior at times seems to interfere with instruction, teachers are willing to warn some students repeatedly rather than discipline them and risk breaking the friendly atmosphere. In the faculty lounge, teachers talk about a wide variety of social events. Conversation is at a high pitch, preventing some teachers from meeting together quietly. Laughter is continual. When we question several teachers about how they use their autonomy, we are told about how well they work together and how that allows them to develop challenging classroom instruction. Since it is Friday, we are invited by the teachers to join them and their administrators at a local bar after the school day is over.

As we walk around the school, observing classrooms, we see that instruction is being carried out in most cases by teachers standing at the front of the classroom, lecturing, asking questions, and assigning seat work, even though we have been told that teachers at Dewey demonstrate "unique approaches to teaching and learning." We do see some large group instruction, some attempts at collaborative learning, and some situations where students are allowed to work alone or in small groups, although these are by far the minority of cases that we observe. Overall, the school seems to be moving in many different directions in a leisurely fashion. With little real challenge from the teachers, students have adapted themselves to the pace of the school culture. Textbooks remain the basic instructional tool used by teachers, but within the framework provided by the textbooks, their teaching is marked by discretion to do as they please. There are relatively few new teachers at Dewey Junior High School. When asked about the seniority of the faculty, one teacher candidly states that, "No one wants to leave Dewey since we're all professional teachers who have the academic freedom to do pretty much what we want in our classrooms. We are a veteran staff that works well together, one that the administration leaves alone. The principal observes us once a year and schedules a one-hour faculty meeting once a month. Our only problem is that the students could be brighter, but then, you have to look at the neighborhood they come from. I can't think of another school in which I'd rather teach."

The Case of Horace Mann Elementary School

Across town, Horace Mann Elementary School, with an enrollment of 650 students, is located in an upper-middle-class suburb of the city. As we enter the school, the office is easy to find. The halls, void of teachers and students, are silent. Classroom doors are closed. Inside the office two tearful students, with obvious concern in their eyes, sit on a wooden bench opposite the counter, clearly waiting for the principal. The secretary ushers us into the inner office and we are welcomed by the principal. "At Horace Mann Elementary School, students know that they must study hard to meet the standards of the school, and that they have to behave according to the school conduct code," says the principal. "The teachers work hard to teach the curriculum and maintain orderly classrooms." A preplanned schedule of visits to particular teachers is handed to us, and we are warned to keep to the schedule, since the teachers are expecting us and have planned special programs.

As we walk down the halls, a few children are standing quietly outside classrooms. We are struck by how each classroom is arranged in much the same way—desks in rows, teachers and teachers' desks in front, and the school rules and classroom schedules posted on the right side of the chalkboard under the American flag. After visiting two classrooms, we accompany a teacher to recess duty, where we watch third, fourth, and fifth grade children explode onto the playground. We go to the teacher's room for a cup of coffee, with hopes of entering into conversation with teachers not on recess duty. There are only two teachers present—one absorbed in correcting papers, and the other reading the newspaper. The other teachers have either remained in their classrooms or are meeting with the principal. No effort is made to talk to us.

After recess, our schedule takes us to the classrooms of two fifth grade teachers. Both not only use the same textbooks, but also share an essentially "lecture-test" approach to learning. As we leave the second classroom, the teacher comes up to us and says "The entire curriculum for all grades has been organized and structured by the principal so that he knows what is being taught in every classroom. At the first faculty meeting of each school year, curriculum materials and subject schedules, developed by the principal and central office supervisors, are handed out and explained by the principal." "How does the principal ensure that teachers follow the rigid routine?" we inquire. "Every Friday, lesson plans for the following week must be turned in to the principal for review before the teachers can leave for the weekend. Moreover, the teacher evaluation system implemented by central office supervisors reinforces the principal's judgments and actions," replies the teacher. In the classrooms we have visited, students have been quiet, attentive, and focused on their school work. There is little opportunity for students to leave their seats and move around the classroom. Misbehavior is dealt with quickly; if students do not obey a warning, they are either sent to stand in the hall or to the office to see the principal, depending on the severity of their behavior. Most teachers are friendly and show both warmth and concern for their students, but nevertheless they manage to keep tight control of their classrooms.

We leave Horace Mann Elementary School at the conclusion of the day with several teachers. They remark that they feel that teaching at Horace Mann is little more than just classroom teaching. The principal's procedures and program are to be followed to the letter. When teachers have suggested changes in curriculum to the principal, they have been told to keep to the program of study since it prepares the students in the basics, which is what the parents want. When one teacher used several reading texts in addition to the basal text, she was transferred at the end of the year to a less desirable school. The teachers that we are talking to indicate that they have learned their lesson from this.

Analysis and Discussion. The two case studies you have just read are interesting because the faculties and principals of both schools, if asked, would consider their schools to be effective, as do teachers and administrators in most schools in the United States. Though the two schools are in the same school district, they are obviously quite different philosophically. John Dewey Junior High School is organized to meet the individual needs of the teachers, while Horace Mann Elementary School focuses on the organizational goals set by the principal.

John Dewey Junior High School is an easygoing school in which students and teachers are left pretty much to themselves. A wide range of student behavior is permitted in the corridors. Other than using the same textbooks, individual teachers have a great deal of autonomy in developing their individual instructional programs. Some faculty members have clearly used that autonomy to become highly effective classroom teachers. On the whole, however, there do not appear to be high academic expectations for the students, and teachers have not used their autonomy to study the possibility of developing a challenging middle school program. Monthly faculty meetings are endured rather than perceived as an opportunity for teachers to come together to discuss critical educational issues affecting their students. The principal perceives the school as staffed by professionals who do not need to be challenged to use their autonomy and capabilities to restructure Dewey Junior High School; consequently, supervision is marked by a nondirective approach. Teachers like one another at John Dewey. Although they have developed a high degree of positive interpersonal relationships both inside and outside the school, they cannot be said to have been as successful in carrying out a challenging educational program.

Horace Mann Elementary School is a demanding, highly structured school. The parents whose children attend the school know that their children go to school and learn. They also believe, as does the principal, that this is made possible by the school's emphasis on behaving according to the rules of the school. To meet the high expectations parents have for their children, teachers implement a rigorous instructional program in their classrooms that has been designed by the principal. Classrooms are well organized, with desks in neat rows. Children are quiet at Horace Mann and know what happens to them when they misbehave. Similarly, teachers know that they are expected to carry out the curriculum as approved by the principal. Supervision is directive and carried out directly by the principal, whose efforts are supported by the central administration. There is little communication among the teachers, who come to school in the morning, teach the children assigned to their classrooms, and then leave for home. Although the teachers focus on instruction by implementing a regimented program, the teachers do not really participate in the development of the educational program for their classroom or the school. As was the case with John Dewey Junior High School, Horace Mann Elementary School would appear to be ineffective in some significant ways. Whatever else may take place at Horace Mann, it is obvious that neither teachers nor students can be said to be empowered.

Inquiry as Research: A Case Study

The "accelerated schools" movement has been an important reform effort in American education in recent years. The following case provides an outstanding description of what is entailed in an accelerated school:

> Hollibrook Accelerated Elementary School in the Spring Branch Independent School District of Houston is situated

in a neighborhood that is dominated by several large govern-
ment- subsidized apartment complexes. The school sprawls
across several acres and is a maze of hallways, corridors,
temporary classrooms, and outside walkways. . . .

As students begin to arrive on campus, most come on
foot from the surrounding neighborhood. Over thirty-five
countries of national origin are represented here, with more
than 90% of the students coming from Hispanic immigrant
families. More than 85% of the students enter the school
speaking no English, and many have never been to school
before. Ninety-one percent of the students are on the free and
reduced lunch and breakfast program at school. . . .

[Hollibrook] is very large—over 1,000 students plus 100
faculty members. Its children are poor and don't speak
English . . . they performed in the bottom 25th percentile on
district administered standardized tests. Student turnover
amounted to 104% with many students cycling in and out
several times during the course of the year. Both student
and staff morale was low, and discipline and vandalism
were major concerns. Few parents and family members came
to school to attend PTA meetings or conferences. The new
principal . . . and her teachers decided that something dras-
tic had to be done to improve things at school. After a year
of careful study, discussion, and reflection, the vehicle of
change they selected . . . was the Accelerated Schools Project.

In adopting the Accelerated Schools Project, the school
expanded its definition of community and the roles that
each member of the community plays in the decision-making
process. The Hollibrook family—composed of teachers, staff,
administration, students, parents and local community,
began the process of acceleration by taking stock of the
present situation and formulating a unified vision of what
Hollibrook should be in the future. The unity of purpose
which resulted from these activities, as the present was
compared to that vision, induced changes that have made
a dramatic difference in the lives of Hollibrook students and
faculty.

The school community prioritized their areas of challenge and selected several for immediate attention. Task forces were established for each of these priority areas, which included school improvement, staff development, curriculum, and parent involvement, and they began to meet weekly to discuss the challenges and to utilize an . . . inquiry approach to define and solve them. A Steering Committee was elected to link the task forces together into a shared governance system. Decision-making at the school was informed by research and school data with the children as the central focus. After three years of participation in the process of acceleration, Hollibrook can look with pride at many notable successes.

The Accelerated Schools goal of broadened community participation is exemplified at Hollibrook. As a result of the efforts of the Parent Involvement Committee, which included teacher home visits and outreach projects, parents and family members are now a visible presence at Hollibrook and serve in many roles. . . .

There is a living room, kitchen and dining room, completely furnished. The teacher inside explains to you that this is the newcomers' center, where students newly arrived from Central and South America learn English in a setting which also enables them to learn about the customs and culture of their new country. The older bilingual children spend time in the room as peer tutors for the new children and help them adjust to their new home. . . .

[One class of] third grade students are all actively engaged in their academic tasks. Some are working in small groups with a student facilitator. Others are working with the teacher or teacher's aide. There are also two student observers from the local university's teacher education program in the room. . . . Another group of students is working on a math work sheet entitled, "Penguin Power Math." Although there is much activity in the room, the noise level is not very high and no one seems to be distracted by other groups. Students are so eager and engrossed that they scarcely notice visitors in their midst. This focus on thematic learning and active and interactive teaching and learning illustrates the enormous success of the Staff Development and Curriculum Task Force as they have focused on the improvement of teaching and learning at the school. . . .

The efforts and hard work of the entire school community at Hollibrook have yielded enormous dividends in two and one- half years. Student and teacher surveys document dramatic increases in self-esteem and morale. Student mobility rates have come down from 104% to 47%. Incidents of vandalism are down by 78%. Student expulsions decreased from five in 1989-90 to zero in 1990-91. The PTA meetings attract from 600 to 800 people. In addition to these important changes, test scores on standardized tests have soared. . . .

As the principal of Hollibrook sums up their experience, she says, "The faculty, with focused vision and effort, turned Hollibrook around in a fashion which is true to the Cinderella fairytale. However, this is no fairytale. The results are due to the valiant efforts of the staff, the students, the parents and the community. There was no infusion of funding to make the difference. It was not the purchasing of new gadgets, textbooks, or the adoption of new programs from publishers. The staff was not replaced. Scores reflecting improved student achievement were not accomplished by exempting the less capable, remediating those who were left behind, or by adding a magnet gifted program to bring in the more capable children from across the district. The Hollibrook story is remarkable because the school community had defied all odds. . . . " (Accelerated Schools Project, 1991, pp. 4-9)

Analysis and Discussion. The case of Hollibrook Elementary School describes how a school faculty, with leadership from its principal, is able to turn around an urban elementary school beset with problems. How did this happen? In the first place, the principal facilitated the discussion by the school community of the needs, values, and aspirations of the teachers and parents, and induced them to discuss the specific problems confronting the school, analyze them, and then develop operational plans for resolving them. In the second place, the empowerment of the faculty by the principal enabled them to work together, develop a sense of common purpose for Hollibrook, and then reach out to the school community for understanding and support. We see that the staff is beginning to take leadership for the resolving problems, producing a kind of shared governance in the school. Using a term from James MacGregor Burns, all of the parties involved have been *elevated* by the new relationships. In the third place, the school community, so often ignored or overlooked by school faculties, has been welcomed in helping to address Hollibrook's challenges and problems. Now there is unity of purpose, both within the school and in the school community. In the fourth place, it is important to note that the principal and faculty were able to agree on adopting a reflective practice—in this case, the Inquiry Process of the Accelerated Schools Program (Accelerated Schools Project, 1991)—to undergird and structure their work. Finally, a critical element of leadership demonstrated by the Hollibrook case is the accomplishment of "intended effects" (Burns, 1979, p. 22). Over the two and a half years that the principal and the members of the faculty and school community of Hollibrook Elementary School have worked together on making the school effective, they have been successful in producing the intended effects that they sought.

Leadership and Followership in a Democracy

The culture of the John Dewey Middle School encourages the professional staff to emphasize its individual needs, motives, and aspirations. The various behaviors of teachers are idiosyncratic and do not focus on collaborative efforts. The principal believes that when teachers have autonomy in their classrooms and close interpersonal relationships in the lounge and at after-school activities, a good school climate has been established. The culture of the Horace Mann Elementary School emphasizes the bureaucratic, and autocratic, standards of the principal and the school district. The principal of Horace Mann believes that when teacher discretion is limited, and district curricular and instructional objectives are followed, the school can best accomplish its mission. When teachers meet those expectations, they are rewarded; when they deviate, they are punished.

In his seminal book *Functions of the Executive*, Chester Barnard (1938) noted that executives need to balance the needs and aspirations of the individuals in an organization with the needs and purposes of the organization (pp. 19-21). The behavior of teachers is *effective* when organizational objectives are met; the behavior of teachers is *efficient* when their individual wants and motives, which undergird organizational goals and objectives, are achieved. At Horace Mann, the behavior of teachers is effective since it is congruent with the expectations of the principal, yet inefficient, since the teachers' individual wants and needs are not satisfied. At John Dewey, the behavior of teachers is efficient, since the individual wants and needs of teachers are satisfied, but ineffective since organizational goals are not achieved. One school is effective without being efficient, the other efficient without being effective. While both efficiency and effectiveness are necessary characteristics for a good organization, it is also important to note that they are not, on their own, sufficient—an organization might well be both efficient and effective, and still be undesirable on normative or moral grounds.

The Hollibrook Elementary School exemplifies a school in which the professional staff's wants and needs are satisfied, while at the same time the needs and objectives of the school are being met. Further, this is taking place in an environment that is clearly ethically acceptable. Organizations such as Hollibrook, in short, are marked by a congruence of efficiency and effectiveness (Hoy & Miskel, 1987, p. 73), and, in fact, are usually marked by a pervading sense of unity as well.

John Goodlad (1984) has argued that in the United States, schools and classrooms, and the teaching and learning that occurs in those schools and classrooms, appear similar until the power relationships among teachers, students, administrators and parents in those schools and classrooms are analyzed. To change the culture of schools such as the John Dewey Middle School and Horace Mann Elementary School, the power relationships must be analyzed and critiqued, and plans of action may be drawn to promote change. Otherwise, the organizations will remain fundamentally the same and continue to be resistant to change. As Sarason (1990) has argued, "Schools will remain intractable to desired reform as long as we avoid confronting (among other things) their existing power relationships. . . . Changing existing power relationships is a necessary condition for reaching goals, but it is not sufficient" (p. 5).

One of the most important factors in creating an effective and efficient school is its leadership. Gardner (1990) has defined leadership as "the process of persuasion or example by which an individual (or leadership team) induces a group to pursue objectives held by the leader or shared by the leader and his or her followers." The principals at John Dewey Middle School, Horace Mann Elementary School, and Hollibrook Elementary School have developed, both consciously and unconsciously, very different power relationships in their respective schools. The behavior of the John Dewey principal might be characterized as laissez-faire and nondirective, intended to create a disengaged school climate; while the behavior of the Horace Mann principal is directive and bureaucratic, creating a relatively closed school climate. Finally, the behavior of the Hollibrook principal is more collegial and democratic and functions to create an open school climate (see Hoy & Miskel, 1987, pp. 93-110). As a consequence of the different power relationships present in each of the three schools, different school learning environments and cultures are created for students and teachers. In a sense, Dewey and Mann are "intractable," but Hollibrook, with its democratic leader and open climate, encourages change in order to meet the needs of students and staff as well as the goals of the school (Hoy & Miskel, p. 73).

Burns has suggested that "leadership over human beings is exercised when persons with certain motives and purposes mobilize, in competition or conflict with others, institutional, political, psychological and other resources so as to arouse, engage, and satisfy the motives of others" (1979, p. 18). In other words, both Burns and Gardner perceive a direct power relationship between leaders and followers, but Burns goes somewhat further, defining leadership as "[inducing] followers to act for certain goals that represent the values and motivations—wants and needs, the aspirations and expectations—of both leaders and followers." Three broad, general types of leadership are identified and discussed by Burns:

> *Transactional Leadership,* in which leaders approach followers to exchange one thing for another.
>
> *Transformational Leadership,* in which leaders and followers raise each other to higher levels of morality and motivation.
>
> *Moral Leadership,* in which leaders and followers have common motives, needs, aspirations and values. (pp. 4-5)

The effectiveness and efficiency of leadership are determined, in essence, by the "degree of production of intended effects" (Burns, 1979). The leadership provided by the principals at both John Dewey Middle School and Horace Mann Elementary School is basically transactional in nature and does not create productive schools, in which teachers are elevated to higher levels of motivation. The leadership provided by the principal at Hollibrook Elementary School, on the other hand, is transformational in nature and, by raising the aspirations and motivations of the teachers, has enabled them to develop a school that has produced the intended effects.

In examining the relationship between leaders and followers, Burns (1979) argues that "transforming leadership is a relationship of mutual stimulation and elevation that converts followers into leaders and may convert leaders into moral agents." At Hollibrook Elementary School, the principal was able to induce the teachers, parents, and students to work to restructure the school by confronting critical problems that represented educational values and motivations. Once the problems had been identified and agreed upon, both the leaders and the followers found they had common wants, needs, aspirations, and expectations. As teachers and parents working in committees reflected about the agreed-upon problems, developed courses of action, implemented solutions, and accepted responsibility, they became, in turn, leaders themselves.

Transformational leadership is critical for principals and teachers since so many of the problems confronting education are basically questions of values, ethics, and vision. All too often, the work of educational leaders in our society is conceptualized as little more than managing teacher competence and achievement tests, rather than helping teachers, parents, and students address the critical questions that Dewey and the other progressive educators raised at the turn of the century: What type of education does public education need to provide citizens for our democracy? How do we make schools places where the curiosity of children is challenged? In order to answer these questions, we need to involve teachers, parents, and students in re-ordering the schools, so that they become places in which learning becomes the basis of challenging social practices (see Giroux, 1992, p. 8). Such an environment would require educators to be conscious of the values basic to their pedagogical and political vision.

Reflective Thinking and the Teacher and Administrator

The culture of education in a democracy is one in which the goals are ambiguous, the context of practice so varied that it is almost site-specific, and there is limited agreement about what constitutes the content of professional knowledge (see Schön, 1983, p. 46). In such a culture teachers and administrators need a process by which they can make decisions. Mezirow (1990, p. 1) has suggested that individuals make meaning of experience by interpretation, and consequently use it as a guide to decision making. Meaning is structured in two ways: (a) through meaning *schemes*, which are "sets of related and habitual expectations governing if-then and cause-effect relationships"; and (b) through meaning *perspectives*, which are "structures of assumptions within which new experience is assimilated." The schemes and perspectives control what we learn. Reflection on prior learning is an "assessment of how, or why we have perceived thought, or felt, or acted." John Dewey, as was noted earlier in this book, believed that reflection should be taught to all citizens in a democracy (see Dewey, 1933, p. 9). Furthermore, he argued that "active, persistent, and careful consideration of any belief or supposed form of knowledge in the light of the grounds that support it and the further conclusions to which it tends, constitutes reflective thought." Mezirow's concept of reflection differentiates between *thoughtful* action, where one draws upon past experience, and *reflective* action, which is based on critical assessment of assumptions and presuppositions.

Two other useful concepts related to reflective thinking are also introduced by Mezirow: *instrumental learning* and *communicative learning* (1990, pp. 7-9). Instrumental learning occurs when educators attempt tasks (for example, developing the curriculum for a new content area or determining instructional methodologies). In instrumental learning, the first step is to assess one's individual and personal assumptions regarding curriculum and instruction. Many times such a process results in solutions in which other people are controlled and their work areas must be manipulated. Judging the validity of such solutions becomes important. Validity can be provided by two factors: (a) informed consensus regarding the logic of the analysis going into the problem solving; and (b) the empirical data about whether the solution solves the problem (that is, what Burns calls the intended effects).

Communicative learning refers to understanding meaning. Here teachers and principals attempt to understand what is meant by the language and writing of others. They are trying to fit unfamiliar or novel ideas and concepts into perspectives and experiences that have meaning for themselves.

Kitchener and King (discussed in Mezirow, 1990, pp. 159-166) have developed a reflective judgment model, which can be used for better understanding the critical assumptions that individuals use in problem solving. The authors differentiate stages of problem solving and how the "assumptions about sources and certainty of knowledge" vary and develop. In other words, what Kitchener and King actually provide us with is a model for classifying the epistemological sophistication of the individual. The seven stages of problem solving (that is, of epistemological strategies) offered by Kitchener and King are:

Stage One: Knowing is characterized by a concrete, single-category belief system.

Stage Two: Individuals assume that while truth is ultimately accessible, it may not be directly and immediately known to everyone.

Stage Three: Individuals acknowledge that some areas of truth are temporarily inaccessible, even for those in authority. In other areas they maintain the belief that authorities know the truth.

Stage Four: The uncertainty of knowing is initially acknowledged ... and usually attributed to limitations of the knower.

Stage Five: Individuals believe that knowledge must be placed within a context. This assumption derives from the understanding that interpretation plays a role in what a person perceives.

Stage Six: Individuals . . . . believe that knowing is uncertain and that knowledge must be understood in relationship to the context from which it is derived.

Stage Seven: Although individuals . . . . believe that knowing is uncertain and subject to interpretation, they also argue that epistemically justifiable claims can be made about the better or best solution to the problem under consideration. (Mezirow, 1990, pp. 159-166)

Since many of the problems educators face are "ill structured" (Mezirow, 1990, p. 166), it is important that teachers and principals recognize the value of reflective thinking as a process of solving problems, making decisions, and setting direction. However, teachers and administrators enter problem-solving groups with different assumptions about what is known and how decisions should be made. Leaders must understand the stages of the reflective judgment model that individual group members may be on, and be able to assist the group in developing decisions that are acceptable to all members of the group and will also meet the goals of the school.

The ill-structured problems that confront American education and its schools require the best thinking on the part of parents, teachers, and administrators. A critical element in this process is leadership. When that leadership is transformational, leaders and followers can work together, elevate each other, and successfully achieve educational reform.

Propositions for Reflection and Consideration

1. In efficient and effective schools, the needs, wants, and aspirations of the teachers, as well as the needs of the school, are achieved.
2. The key to educational reform is understanding the power relationships that exist between students, teachers, administrators, and parents that inform and control the behavior in schools.
3. The same factors that enable students to grow and develop also enable teachers to grow and develop.
4. The climate of a school affects how teachers behave. It describes how teachers perceive their work environment. An open climate fosters collegial and supportive relationships; a closed climate fosters a directive and restrictive relationship.
5. The values and motivations that enable leaders to induce followers to act for goals are the same for leaders.
6. By transformational leadership a principal elevates the teachers and himself or/herself to higher levels of morality and motivation.
7. Reflective thinking is a process that parents, teachers, and administrators can use for problem solving and decision making.
8. Since decisions resulting from reflective thinking may affect others, decision-making groups can demonstrate validity for decisions by providing informed consensus and empirical data about whether the solution solves the problem.
9. School problem solving is enhanced when leaders and followers understand that different individuals act upon assumptions from different stages of the reflective judgment model.

The School as Community
and the School in the Community

The role of the community in making the schools vital is just as important as the role of the school itself. For in a community where schools are looked upon as isolated institutions, as a necessary convention, the school will remain largely so in spite of the most skillful methods of teaching. But a community that demands something visible from its schools, that recognizes the part they play in the welfare of the whole . . . that uses the energies and interest of its youthful citizens, not simply controlling their time until they are prepared to be turned out as citizens—such a community will have social schools, and whatever its resources, it will have schools that develop community spirit and interests.

John and Evelyn Dewey (1962, p. 128)

What the best and wisest parent wants for his own child, that must the community want for all of its children.

John Dewey (1943, p. 7)

The Case of Broadbent Middle School

Northport is best known as the site of the national headquarters of a large manufacturing firm, and its economy and social life have been closely intertwined with the firm for decades. In recent years the manufacturing firm has fallen on hard times, and each year, layoffs have increased. In this environment, funding and support for the schools have been growing more and more problematic, and there is a strong movement in the community to drastically cut the school's budget.

Alice Meere is the principal of Broadbent Middle School, which is one of two middle schools in Northport. The faculty at Broadbent Middle School is composed of highly educated professionals, who have been repeatedly recognized by accreditation teams for their subject matter competence. Under Alice's leadership, the faculty has willingly accepted responsibility for developing new courses of study and academic programs and believe that they have been very successful in their efforts.

As a way of protecting Broadbent Middle School, Alice has decided to hold a series of public meetings in the auditorium, where teachers, school administrators, and local political leaders will be able to present arguments and evidence about the fiscal needs of the schools in Northport. The first of these meetings took place on a Tuesday evening and, although well attended, was not quite the success on which Alice had counted.

The turnout at the Tuesday meeting was well beyond anyone's expectations, but the crowd present was far more critical of the schools than Alice or any of her staff had expected. Parents and other members of the community challenged the competence of the teachers, the content of the curriculum, the lack of adequate vocational programs, and what they perceived as exorbitant teacher and administrator salaries. It was clear that many people in the community were angry with the schools and felt that they had no input into important decisions that affected their children and the way in which their taxes were spent. Alice was afraid that the public meeting she scheduled may have done far more harm than good, by providing a public forum for attacking the schools, and was unsure about what her next step should be.

Analysis and Discussion. The case of Northport is far from unusual, as budgets and resources are stretched to and even beyond their limits. What is interesting in this particular case is how out of touch with the community the principal and teachers seem to have been. Although they no doubt anticipated that concerns would be voiced, they did not realize how angry parents and other members of the community were with a whole host of issues related to the school. Further, members of the community had come to see the school system not as "our" system, but rather as an imposed and somewhat alien system controlled by the professionals, which was costing them a great deal of money and not providing the services they desired. In other words, the school-community bond in Northport had been effectively severed. The challenge facing Alice Meere and her staff, as well as other educators in the school system, is less the immediate problem of the budget than the more general, and far more significant, problem of developing support in the community.

The School/Community Interface

Until the last quarter of the nineteenth century, the family was the major socializing force in the lives of its members. A wide variety of functions was provided for, to a significant degree, by the family: business (the home was the center of work for most Americans), education (parents were responsible for the education of their children), vocational training (children received job training from their parents), religion (families supplemented the church in terms of both religious instruction and religious practice), correction (families were responsible for disciplining their members), and welfare (care was provided for all members, young and old) (see Demos, 1970). As American society became increasingly urbanized and industrialized, and as the population of the society became more diverse, state governments gradually began to view education as a means of carrying out a variety of social agendas. The emergence of tax-supported, public educational systems, initially in New England and rapidly spreading through the Old Northwest, led to a number of important questions about the role, nature, and purposes of such educational institutions. Among the more significant questions with which Americans were faced were: What is the role of education in a democratic society? What are the purposes of the existing reading and writing schools, the academies, and the grammar schools? Should the schools maintain the status quo and preserve the groups controlling society? Or, rather, should the schools be charged with the responsibility of improving the general welfare of all the people? These questions had actually been implicitly addressed earlier in American history, by no less a figure than Thomas Jefferson, who was the first American leader to seek to "establish public education as an instrument for the realization of democracy and for furthering social reform," (Sizer, 1984, p. 71). More important for our purposes, these same questions are still being debated as we move toward the twenty-first century. As teachers, administrators, parents, and other citizens seek to come to grips with such questions, they need to reflect on their own values, determine individual and group positions, and then develop the kinds of schools and schooling that will meet not only the wants and aspirations of the youth in their classrooms but also the needs of the society.

In Chapter 4, the principals of John Dewey Middle School and Horace Mann Elementary School had relatively conservative (although quite different) views of education. The role of the school, for both of these leaders, was to preserve the status quo, though admittedly in very different ways. These two principals had decided that the values undergirding the current school culture had been achieved at great cost and should not be changed precipitously, and also that any problems would be resolved gradually and in due course.

Freire (1972, pp. 2-4) has discussed the conservative role played by the school in a slightly different context. He argues that dominant cultures (for instance, in contemporary American society, the Anglo-American culture), tend to overlook the wants and needs of the dominated cultures that coexist with the dominant culture. Freire suggests that schools, as social institutions involved in the maintenance of the status quo, generally function to impose the values of the dominant culture on dominated cultural groups in the society. Basic literacy skills, such as reading and writing, can thus sometimes become for dominated groups acts of memorization and repetition, rather than acts of reflection on meaning and critical translation into the child's own culture. This need not be the case, of course, and when the latter takes place, education becomes transforming, not only to individuals but also for both the dominant and dominated cultures. Such transformative educational experiences, however, remain relatively uncommon and are unlikely to be found in either John Dewey Middle School or Horace Mann Elementary School.

The principal of the Hollibrook Elementary School has a more progressive view of education and appears to be open to the wants and demands of the various groups that comprise the school community. Hollibrook was confronted with problems that required new curricula, new instructional approaches, and most important, new power relationships between teachers and parents, between teachers and administrators, between teachers and students, and between the school and the community. The quality of the relationship that develops between a school and the community it serves determines to a large degree the success or failure of that school. With this background in mind, we turn now to three case studies in which the relationship between a school and its community plays a central role.

The Case of Thayer High School

The example of Thayer High School is an especially useful one here. The case of Thayer is really the case of Dr. Dennis Littky, a highly successful principal of a nationally acclaimed middle school on Long Island, who moved to Winchester, New Hampshire, to reflect upon his life and, quite unexpectedly, became the principal of the community's high school. The story of Dennis Littky and Thayer High School is presented below:

> Winchester's 3,600 people live in a wide, rectangular tract of land rounded off by soft green hills that rise like bread loaves from the flat center of town. Though it's a town of subtle enough natural beauty to have once been considered, a couple of centuries ago, as the home of Dartmouth College, today it's one of the poorest towns in the state. A few years ago, a New Hampshire newspaper referred to Winchester as "a little piece of Appalachia," and if anybody objected, they didn't write in to say so. A lot of people work at the shearing tannery in town, others at the paper mills down by the river, and, according to county welfare figures,

quite a few don't work at all. The high school was said to have a dropout rate of 20%, but those inside the school say they knew it to be much higher.

Along the main street, which is a north-south state highway, the covered sidewalks offer a tempting spot for townspeople to sit during the day and often on into the night. Such a scene is probably what provoked the popular description of Winchester as a "cowboy town." Or maybe it is the unbridled nature of the town where frustrated police chiefs and town managers come and go with remarkable speed. The summer that Dennis [Littky] came to town, local youths, perhaps trying to bait the overzealous new police chief, enjoyed the habit of sitting out on the porch of the local tavern, smoking joints and drinking beer. Or inscribing zigzags and doughnuts in the pavement of the four corners with the rear wheels of their fast cars.

"Winchester was thought of as a kind of joke," Dennis said recently. "I'd go somewhere and people would laugh: "You actually *live* in Winchester?" And I began to see that people in town made jokes about how crummy the school system was: "Oh, you can't spell? You must have gone to Thayer!"

Education was his specialty; he thought maybe he could offer something, so he joined the PTA, which at the time had 15 members, all of whom were women. It was the beginning of the end of his retreat.

"I could see that one of the worst things about Winchester was the people's self-image. Everyone I met was really a good person, yet because of the power of that negative image, these wonderful people didn't come through." The regional daily paper rarely featured news of Winchester, which ego-bereft Winchesterites took to mean, "Who cares?"

. . . In the spring of 1980, the Thayer principal resigned. Judy, Marcia and others in town urged Dennis to try for the job. By that time they not only knew the extent of his background, but also had witnessed the effect he'd already had on the town. Judy put ballot boxes around town, asking for the townspeople's opinions of what the high school needed and urging Dennis as the town's choice. . . .

When Dennis showed up for his interview with the school board, he wore the same corduroys and short-sleeved shirt that he usually wore when he dressed up for PTA meetings and to go to Concord. "I knew these people. I saw them all the time. I would have felt stupid getting all dressed up. In the interview, the school board asked me about a dress code, and I asked them for me or for the kids. They said, 'For you.' So I said, 'What you see is what you get.' The next day I heard the line all over town. It almost cost me the job."

"I wanted the job so badly. Once I started thinking about it, the possibilities were very exciting. I knew that the school was in horrible shape, but it was *my* town. I think I would have been hurt and embarrassed if I hadn't gotten it."

The vote on the school board was close, 3-2, giving Dennis the job. He took a salary of $22,000 . . . and plunged in. Even before he'd set foot in the school, Dennis made the magnanimous statement to the local newspaper: Thayer was going to be one of the best schools in the state.

Thayer High School was built in 1922, in the style of almost every other school built in this country during that era; a square, two-story brick building, barren of adornment inside or out. Except for the junior high school addition, there have been no substantial alterations made since 1922. The classrooms are large with tall windows and high, pressed-metal ceilings. The hallways, with exposed plumbing strung overhead, are lined with olive drab lockers that make it hard for three to pass abreast. When Dennis first came, the walls needed paint, especially to cover the obscenities that covered the bathroom stalls. Attendance was poor, the dropout rate was higher than 20 percent, and the class that graduated the June before sent only four of its 48 seniors to college. . . . At Thayer there were pregnant girls even in the ninth grade; other kids had no apparent home. Broken homes were nearly as common as whole ones. . . .

The soul-searching entries in his journal vanished, replaced by long lists of What Needs to Be; high on the list was communication between parents and school and town. He scheduled conferences with parents, something that had never been done before, and private bets were placed among veteran teachers: "He'll never get parents to come through that door," they wagered. But, even if he had to go pick them up, he got nine out of ten of them there to talk about what they wanted for their kids. Likewise he scheduled talks with every kid in the school. "I asked each one of them what they were going to do after they got out. Most of them said, 'Get a job.' But when I asked them what kind, none of them knew. They didn't have the faintest idea!"

He sniffed around town for people with the kind of qualifications he looks for in a teacher, namely, excellence . . . . But he found that there were teachers willing to sacrifice pay; the gap was bridged by Dennis' enthusiasm. . . . Though state funds available to Winchester were paltry, Dennis knew that there were grants available, that they need only apply. He trained teachers to fill out the tedious grant proposals and did many himself. "What they're looking for when they're giving out grants are good ideas and I'm never short on ideas."

"The apprenticeship program provides about $50,000 worth of free instruction for the school," a Star volunteer assessed. "A lot of what Dennis is aiming at is designed to bring things to the school that don't cost the school anything. He does it by enlisting the aid of the community." Indeed, one of Dennis's strengths is that he gets money out of nowhere. "We can get it if we believe we can. People say, 'God, how did he do that?' And I sometimes get criticized for my budget because the way I move money around seems almost mysterious. It would be great if we had resources within the school. But we don't. So we can gather resources through the apprenticeship program, for one. We have apprentices at a drafting company with facilities we couldn't hope to have. But there are other things, like our library is very inadequate. Also transportation, especially with the comings and goings of the apprentices, is a real problem. I bought a car, a used station wagon, for the school. It helps tremendously, moving a couple of kids around when you don't need a big bus. But I was criticized for that."

Last year the school heard about a building that could be had for free. "All we had to do was move it," Dennis says. A crew of students and teachers took it down and rebuilt it behind the high school. It is now the science building, complete with furniture and its own heating plant.

A visitor to the high school might see Dennis hugging students or rooting for them like a cheerleader. He's not their buddy but a friend, and they know that. His first year, when everyone in town knew him as Dennis, he had to impress on them the importance of everyone calling him Dr. Littky. He has a sternness that comes out at the appropriate times, his playfulness evaporating. . . .

At Thayer it [vandalism] is a problem, but a diminishing one since Dennis took over. Enlisting a lot of student help, Dennis fixed up the building the best he could with the money available. "The girls' bathroom was really the pits," Dennis assesses. "I got the girls together and told them I was willing to fix it up, but if it got bad again, I'd have to hire a monitor. So they cleaned it up, they sanded it, they painted it. It was a process everyone was involved in. It's *their* bathroom."

In a school where the dropout rate was high and attendance a problem, in some cases simply because the parents keep the kids out for their convenience, suspension and expulsion are not adequate disciplinary tools. "I don't have great things over them. I can throw a student out, lower his grade, but we've got to make those things important. If a kid has skipped school, what good does it do to keep him out of school? A lot of parents aren't even home during the day. That's putting them back on the streets. I'd rather keep them in and work with them. When I start to see that I've done everything possible for a kid, offered him all kinds of options and the kid still doesn't respond, and I see that it's hurting the atmosphere of the school, then its time for that kid to step out."

Dennis is presently checking into the possibility of setting up a work crew to which offending students can be assigned, working on town roads, town projects. "Everyone at Thayer feels a part of a team effort," points out an observer. By making every member of the faculty feel that his or her role has a significant impact on the school, Dennis has created very cooperative, strong staff that cares very much what happens to Thayer. . . .

Not everyone backs him. Some blame the problems that still hover over Thayer on Dennis. Some people are still grumpy about his appearance. But this year 16 members of the graduating class went on to college, more than four times that went the year before he came. The dropout rate has slowed to 5%. And the Apprenticeship Program is to be the focus of a conference that will be held in Winchester in October, when once again educators from around the country will come to see what Dennis has done. (Clark, 1983)

Analysis and Discussion. Dennis Littky is a transformational leader who based his operational plans to restructure an inefficient and ineffective high school on specific, articulated, and shared values. He was concerned about the education of *all* students. He believed that education had to meet the needs and wants of the students, and he actively involved students, staff, and parents in his planning since he realized that Thayer High School was part of the much larger social system of Winchester. Consequently, he was able to provide a vision to the staff at Thayer High School about what the school could become. His enthusiasm and sense of direction elevated them, as well as the students and their parents, to levels of behavior previously deemed impossible.

Dr. Littky was an integral part of Winchester. In living there, he could say that Winchester was *his* town, giving him a degree of credibility. He perceived that Winchester was disintegrating, and that there was a negative sense of community that was detrimental not only to Winchester as a whole but, more important, to Thayer High School. As he began, with others in the community, to develop a shared set of values and commitments that was to provide a foundation for the high school, he knew that his credibility would be sorely taxed, particularly by those who feared change.

Thayer High School, until Littky's assumption of the principalship, was isolated from the community, organizations, and local groups. The Apprenticeship Program was an attempt to make Thayer a part of the community and the community a part of Thayer. A critical element of the restructuring of Thayer High School was reviving its relationships with the larger social system of Winchester.

Littky also realized that change of the proportion required by Thayer would inevitably result in conflict. Conflict, for Littky, was part of the democratic process, and was to be expected.

The Case of the Fenton Public Schools

Fenton is a city of 30,000 people on Sebastian Bay, 200 miles northwest of the state capital. It is the only city in Fenton County, and its schools are reasonably well funded by state standards, being above average in the per pupil State Equalized Valuation (SEV), as a consequence of the presence of a large cement factory, several lumber mills, and various other businesses located in Fenton, which is the center of commerce and banking in the county. There are, in addition to the city of Fenton, five rural townships in the county, all relatively poor in comparison with Fenton. The five townships all rely for educational funding primarily on their agricultural base. Each of the townships supports a relatively modern K-8 school, and all of the high school students in the county attend either Fenton High School or St. Michael's, the local parochial high school. The construction of the five township elementary schools has created high levels of school debt for each township. The K-8 programs in the township schools are relatively weak due to their inability to attract quality teachers, low per pupil expenditures, and, at least according to many of the teachers in these schools, relatively low educational expectations on the part of parents for their children.

Fenton High School has an enrollment of 1,300 students—700 from the city and 600 from the townships. Over the years, a comprehensive educational program has been developed that has met the perceived needs of the students from the city as well as the townships. Of particular note are the college preparatory and vocational education programs. Both are tied to programs at the Fenton Community College, which is part of the state community college system.

Until recently Fenton High School has had sufficient space to provide quality education for the wide range of city and township students. Faced with increasing enrollments, though, the Fenton Board of Education has decided that if the present programmatic depth and breadth, to which parents have become accustomed, is to be continued, a new high school must be built. Since the new high school would be built primarily to serve the increasing numbers of students from the townships (the projected number of students from Fenton showing no growth), the Board of Education is aware of the possible resistance from Fenton residents, many of whom would have serious reservations about paying for a new high school for the children of township residents.

The superintendent of schools studied the situation and recommended that the Board of Education ask each of the five township school boards to schedule a vote to approve annexation to the Fenton Public Schools, thereby ensuring the enrollment at Fenton High School. In return for each township's giving up control over its elementary school, the Fenton Public Schools would assume the school debt of each township, bring the physical plants and school staffs up to the standards of the Fenton Public Schools, and agree to appoint one member from the five township school boards to the Fenton Board of Education. After much public discussion and debate, the townships agreed to call for the vote. Much to everyone's surprise, each of the townships voted overwhelmingly in favor of annexation, and the Fenton Public Schools grew from 3,000 to 6,000 students, and from an area of 12 square miles to 550.

Realizing that with the vote school community relations had changed drastically, and that five predominantly rural communities were now an integral part of the city school district, the superintendent, with the approval of the Board of Education implemented a community school program. The program was designed to provide each elementary school in the new school district school with a formal decision-making process and a means of communication with the central administration and governing bodies. The community school program had three objectives:

1. to provide the youth and adults of a school with after-school recreation programs;
2. to provide adult education courses at the school; and
3. to provide a process by which the principal, teachers, and parents were responsible for managing their school; members of a school community could discuss their wants and needs; and requests for action could be transmitted to either the school board or city council, whichever was appropriate.

Analysis and Discussion. The Fenton Public Schools had more than an educational problem when annexation was approved by the five township school districts. The effectiveness and efficiency of the new school district would depend to a large degree upon the process of value generation in the five townships, as well as in the city of Fenton itself. All organizations and citizens would be a part of that value generation, either consciously or unconsciously. The school leadership needed to find a sense of shared values, or had to help create it. There were shared values when the townships were independent, but new values would supplant them as new interactive relationships came into being. The superintendent, however, was concerned that when the new school district was created, township autonomy might become dependent upon the city of Fenton, creating a negative relationship of the sort described by Freire.

The superintendent realized that the new value system generated would be critical to success. As Gardner (1990) has written:

If it is healthy and coherent, the community imparts a coherent value system. If it is fragmented or sterile or degenerate, lessons are taught anyway—but not lessons that heal and strengthen. It is a community and culture that hold the individual in a framework of values; when the framework disintegrates, individual value systems disintegrate. (p. 113)

The township communities were homogeneous and traditional in nature, and experienced little change from one generation to the next, whereas the newly created Fenton School District was heterogeneous and now confronted with the likelihood of rapid change.

As a result, the superintendent recommended to the school board a community school program similar to that developed by the Mott Foundation from 1930 to 1980 (see Totten, 1970). The program provided a means for parents, teachers, students, and citizens to meet for recreational, educational, social, and political purposes. However, understandably in the Fenton case, more emphasis was placed on the third objective. Theoretically, it would provide each school community with the power to manage its own school, as well as impact the Fenton School Board and its own township government. Similarly, the Mott Community Schools program envisioned that social agencies, churches, governmental units, service clubs, families, labor and industrial groups, communication media, and any other groups would contribute to the community school (Totten, p. 4). Such contributions would help to achieve the following anticipated outcomes for both the community and individuals residing in the community:

- better understanding of social trends;
- reduction of poverty;
- improved cultural tone;
- reduction of school dropouts;
- improved health and safety;
- reduction of delinquency and crime;
- better employment;
- improved level of literacy; and
- other individual and community improvement.

The school would thus be the "catalytic agent" in accomplishing the shared purposes of the community. The role of the school itself was expanded to include the following functions:

- expectant mothers receive instruction in prenatal care and in planning for parenthood;
- infants receive health checkups of a clinical nature;
- preschool children get ready for the experience of kindergarten;
- undernourished children receive wholesome breakfasts;
- children and youth, during optional periods, engage in a variety of enrichment activities, give expression to their creative talents, and engage in wholesome cultural, social, recreational and service activities;
- school dropouts are reclaimed through personalized programming;
- some adults learn to read, write, and acquire other basic skills, and other adults study in the fields of learning of their choice;
- men and women displaced by automation or forced to rely on public aid can retrain and acquire new marketable skills;
- mothers learn how to purchase, prepare, and conserve food economically as well as construct, repair and launder clothing;
- referrals are made to other agencies for help with specific needs;
- community leaders are discovered and developed;
- people of all races and all socioeconomic backgrounds work, study and play together on an equal basis; and
- older citizens are reclaimed and learn that they are still needed. (Totten, pp. 6-7)

The community school program implemented in the Fenton Public Schools was an attempt to reach out and develop new interactive relationships between the public schools and their communities— one that would create a positive and supportive value structure for the new school district.

The Case of Central City Middle School

The Central City Middle School had been the old high school prior to the construction of the new high school. Modifications for a middle school had been made in the old structure, but 40 years of being *the* high school were too much to overcome. Now there were 900 students in a building designed to hold 1,200. The building was more than adequate, but many of the homes in the surrounding community were run-down and had been converted to multifamily occupancy. Several high-rise tenements had been constructed over the past several years. City reports described the area as lower SES, with a rising crime rate.

One day the teachers at Central City Middle School were talking animatedly in the teachers' lounge about how difficult it was to teach the children in their classrooms. Myriad problems were touched upon in the discussion: single-parent families, drug addiction, teenage pregnancies, child abuse, the never-ending need to discipline, the lack of student motivation, unconcerned parents, low attendance at PTO, and so on. Peter said he thought that Central City Middle School was becoming a fortress in the middle of a hostile neighborhood. Mary agreed with the shopping list of problems, but added that she felt the safest part of each 24-hour day for the students was when they were in school. Ann said that the growing number of problems almost made it appear that parents did not care for their children and their education, but then she concluded by disagreeing with her own argument. She noted that parents were sending their best children to Central City Middle School. Peter picked up on that point, indicating that maybe, just as the teachers needed help with all the problems swirling around each child that affected their behavior, parents also needed help. Just at that moment, one of the counselors, who had been listening attentively, challenged the group by asking them to sit down and talk the situation over with some parents and other members of the community. When the issue was presented to the principal, she was supportive and put the issue on the agenda for the next faculty meeting. Although many of the teachers did not feel that scheduling meetings with the parents and community representatives would work, others thought the idea might help the middle school program and agreed to give the meetings a try. The principal supported the idea strongly and indicated that she would help set up the meetings.

Analysis and Discussion. Many times the reluctance of parents to become involved with teachers in trying to address their children's school problems is the result of the negative school experiences that the parents themselves had as children. Still, the enthusiasm of some of the teachers to try working with the parents could be the first step to restructuring a school perceived by some of the faculty as a "fortress in the middle of a hostile neighborhood." It is important to note, as this case makes clear, that one does not need unanimous support for an effort to change the school environment; rather, one only needs the support of a core group of committed individuals willing to give change a chance. The principal's supportive role is often a key facet in such efforts, since it is the principal who will most likely provide communication with and be able to gain support from the central office, as well as providing administrative assistance of various sorts. James Comer, of Yale University, has strongly advocated the need for school personnel to work with parents to "reduce communication and interpersonal problems." He has suggested that too frequently when teacher-parent groups do meet, there is no agreed-upon problem-solving mechanism. Consequently, in attempting to resolve a problem without guidelines, chaos often reigns and mistrust grows, ultimately destroying what started out as a positive effort (Comer, 1980, p. 67).

In Comer's own work with urban schools, specific program goals were identified. These program goals included:

1. to modify the climate—social and psychological—of the school in a way that facilitates learning;
2. to improve the achievements of basic skills, particularly reading and mathematics, at a statistically significant level;
3. to raise motivation for learning, mastery, and achievement in a way which will increase academic and occupational aspiration levels of each child;
4. to develop patterns of shared responsibility and decision-making among parents and staff; and
5. to develop an organizational relationship between child development and clinical services at Yale University and the educational programs in school systems. (Comer, 1980, pp. 67-68)

To achieve these program goals, Comer established a general process, which he has implemented in several school districts, to bring parents into the decision-making process of the school. This process might, for instance, include the following steps in a particular setting:

- an orientation workshop in the summer for parents, teachers, and administrators in order to establish positive relationships and trust;
- to have the workshop participants discuss and analyze school problems, and gain common perspectives;
- to have workshop participants discuss school governance as a process for planning, implementing and evaluating programs;
- to establish an overall Steering Committee of teachers, parents and administrators "to improve the climate of relationships between parents and school staff, among school staff . . . between staff and students, and to improve teaching and curriculum, staff selection and program evaluation";
- social activities are planned by parents and teachers to support the school program;
- a Mental Health Team is established to help teachers manage children with discipline problems; and
- to develop and implement programs by parents and teachers to resolve various school problems. (Comer, 1980, pp. 72-73)

The teachers in Central City Middle school might use similar steps to establish effective working relationships with their parents. In any case, the teachers would be extending the school into the community and in turn bringing parents into a meaningful relationship with teachers and administrators.

The School and the Community: Some Conclusions

For too long a time the educational problems confronting America and its 14,000 school districts have been perceived as fundamentally school problems. Consequently, the attack on those problems has been made primarily by the school forces. The many other organizations, groups, and individuals also responsible for the problems have been denied access to decision making and problem resolution (Sarason, 1990). Sarason has argued that:

> To a significant degree, the major educational problems stem from the fact that educators not only accepted responsibility for schooling but, more fateful, also adopted a stance that essentially said: we know how to solve and manage the problems of schooling in America. Educators did not say: there is much that we do not know, many problems that are intractable to our efforts, and many individuals we are not reaching or helping. (p. 36)

The family of the twenty-first century will not be solely responsible for the functions of business, education, vocational training, religion, correction, and welfare, but will share those responsibilities with other community agencies. Schools cannot be solely responsible for problems from the larger society that are affecting education. All community groups who are also affected by those problems should participate in their discussion, analysis, and resolution. This necessitates a systems approach to problem solving by schools and school districts. Only when educational responsibility is shared can education be reformed.

Propositions for Reflection and Consideration

1. Public education is a process for achieving democracy and furthering social reform.
2. Depending upon the issue, schools can assume either a conservative role (maintaining the status quo) or a progressive role (being a change agent). When they are open to the needs and wants of students, particularly in urban areas, schools need to be progressive.
3. Teachers and administrators need to determine the overall role of the school—conservative or progressive.
4. In effective and efficient schools change is a dynamic, interactive process between a school and its community.

5. Shared values are generated when a school and its community interact. Those shared values undergird and strengthen schools and their programs.

6. When schools are isolated from their communities, their educational programs become ineffective and their culture begins to disintegrate.

7. Educators have accepted responsibility for problems originating in the larger society even though they do not have solutions for them. Those problems affect many other organizations as well. To generate effective and efficient solutions, educators need to use a system approach, in which other organizations share in decision making.

8. The teacher, principal, and superintendent play key roles in developing a positive role for the school in the community.

Values, Ethics, and Reflective Teaching

Ethics is everybody's concern. Scientific problems and scientific theories may from time to time intrigue or arrest all of us, but they are of immediate, practical importance only to a few. Everyone, on the other hand, is faced with moral problems—problems about which, after more or less reflection, a decision must be reached. So everybody talks about values.

Stephen Toulmin (1968)

Ethical Dilemmas and the Professional Educator: Four Case Studies

Horace Mann High School is a medium-sized, urban school with a predominantly African-American and Puerto Rican population. Although nearly 90% of the students enrolled at Horace Mann are children of color, all but 3 of the 32 teachers at the school are white, as is the principal, John Anderson. The school has a generally good reputation in the community, and Mr. Anderson has sought to encourage the teachers at Horace Mann to become more reflective about their teaching. During the course of the school year, individual teachers in the school have, as always, been faced with a variety of ethical dilemmas and have resolved these dilemmas in many different ways. Four cases in particular demonstrate the role and place of reflection in ethical decision making, and we turn now to an examination of these cases.

The Case of Maria Sanchez

James Rafferty has been a math teacher at Horace Mann for 6 years. He enjoys teaching and has a reputation for having high expectations of his students, but also for being fair and fun in class. Early in October one of the sophomores, Maria Sanchez, came up to him at the end of class and asked if she could speak with him privately about something. James hadn't noticed any problems with Maria's work, though she had seemed a bit absentminded recently, and he gladly agreed to meet her later that day, during his free period. He hoped that he might be able to give Maria some advice about whatever was distracting her, and thus improve her classroom performance. Maria came to his office at the agreed-upon time, and told him that she had been upset recently because another teacher, Mr. Swenson, who taught social studies at Horace Mann, had been trying to get her to go out with him, and she didn't want to. James was surprised by what Maria told him, since he knew Dick Swenson very well and couldn't imagine him behaving in such an unprofessional way. Explaining to Maria that he needed some time to think about what she had told him, he asked her to come to his office before classes started the next day.

The more that James thought about what he had heard, the more he doubted Maria's version of events. Maria might easily have misunderstood something that Dick said, or could even be fabricating the whole matter to make up for her own poor academic performance. On the other hand, he was concerned that if he didn't pass on what Maria had told him to the appropriate school authorities, he could himself get into trouble later on. Still, Dick was his friend and he felt that this ought to count for a great deal in a case like this one. He certainly believed that a person was innocent until proven guilty, and was afraid that if a claim of this sort was pursued, it could fairly quickly turn into a "witch hunt" that would hurt Dick unjustly.

Finally, James stopped by Dick's classroom and asked him if they could meet for a drink after school to discuss something. This wasn't at all unusual, and Dick happily agreed to meet James at a local bar about 4 o'clock. When they met, James told his friend about what Maria had told him. Dick denied the whole story vehemently, and asked James to talk to Maria again and challenge her veracity. He suggested that if a bit of pressure was put on Maria, she would "stop all of this nonsense before it all gets out of hand." Although he had some reservations about the wisdom of taking such action, James agreed to do as Dick asked.

James met with Maria the next morning as they had arranged. He indicated that he had some doubts about what she had told him, informed her that he knew Dick Swenson very well and couldn't imagine him asking a student for a date, and told her that if she were making all of this up, she could get in a lot of trouble. Tears welled up in Maria's eyes, but she brushed them away, said that she under-stood and would keep quiet, and left the room. About a week later, James received word that Maria had dropped out of school. He continued to wonder if what he had done had been the right thing, but felt confident that Maria had probably been lying, and was glad that his friend's reputation was safe.

The Case of Amy Griffen

Amy Griffen was an experienced foreign language teacher who had taught French and Spanish at Horace Mann for almost 20 years. This year, as in many years past, she had agreed to take on a student teacher during the fall semester. The student teacher was Mary Andrews, a student at Western College, who was majoring in Spanish with minors in both French and German. An excellent student with outstanding letters of recommendation, Mary was in her second week of student teaching. Thus far, all that she had done was observe Amy teaching and give a single quiz in one of the first year French classes. However, on the Thursday of her second week of student teaching, Amy pulled her aside and told Mary that she had a doctor's appointment across town during third period. She had forgotten to request a substitute, and wanted Mary to cover the third and fourth period classes while she was gone. Mary felt a bit uncomfortable about this, but agreed, since she wanted to be helpful and also since Amy would be one of the people assigning her grade for student teaching. When Amy got back at the start of fifth period, she made a point of reminding Mary that they needed to keep what they had done just between the two of them.

That night, as she began writing in her journal, Mary puzzled over whether to write about what had really happened in class. She didn't want to get her cooperating teacher in trouble, but at the same time, she thought that her supervisor should know what taken place. It would be hard to write the journal without mentioning the best part of the day—and she'd had two really good classes during Amy's absence. She finally called a friend, who was student teaching in a nearby elementary school, to discuss what had happened. Her friend clearly envied her having had control of the class all by herself, but was also concerned that maybe Mary could get in trouble if she didn't report what had happened. Finally, after they discussed it back and forth for almost an hour, Mary decided to call her supervisor at home. She explained what had happened, and stressed that she wasn't complaining or unhappy. Her supervisor was clearly not happy with what had taken place, but said she'd let it go this time. She also told Mary that she was not, under any circumstances, to take charge of a class while Amy was out of the building, and reminded her that she was not yet a certified teacher. Although Mary hadn't kept her word to Amy to be quiet about what had taken place, she felt better now that her supervisor knew about it.

A Case of Cheating

Larry Epstein was a new teacher at Horace Mann. He had taught at another local high school for 2 years, but this was his first at Horace Mann and he wanted to make a good impression on his colleagues and superiors. Larry had been a good student and very much wanted to be a good science teacher, though he knew that the students thought he was far too hard. He believed, though, that he was just maintaining high standards and if half (or more) of his students failed each grading period, it was because they weren't studying hard enough. Just before winter break, Larry gave his Earth Science students, who had been studying geology all year, an especially difficult midterm examination. During second period, Larry noticed that Dale Evans, one of Horace Mann's outstanding football players, kept fidgeting in his seat. Walking over to where Dale was sitting, Larry saw that he had hidden notes up his shirt sleeve. Larry picked up his test paper and told Dale that he was done and should go to the school office and wait for him there. Dale, looking very depressed, did as he was told.

After class, Larry went directly to the office, and asked to speak with Mr. Anderson. He quickly filled Mr. Anderson in on what had taken place in his class, and expected him to be pleased with his vigilance. Instead, Mr. Anderson chastised him for "making such a big issue out of all of this," reminded Larry that Dale was "a good kid" who was probably just out of his league in Larry's class anyway, indicated that Larry's standards were probably too high, reminded Larry that Dale's only chance of getting into college was on an athletic scholarship and that a failing grade could jeopardize such a scholarship, and then asked Larry if he had any problems working with black kids. Larry was very surprised at Mr. Anderson's reaction and said that he'd have to think about what had been said. As he left the principal's office, he told Dale to go ahead and go to his next class.

Larry then went to Ernie Smith's classroom. Ernie was the science department chairperson, and Larry thought that no matter what happened now, Ernie had better be involved. He quickly filled Ernie in, and Ernie agreed to meet him at the end of the school day in the cafeteria. Ernie was fairly supportive, to Larry's relief, and had brought with him a copy of the NEA "Code of Ethics." He pointed out one passage in particular to Larry: "The educator shall not on the basis of race, color, creed, sex, national origin, marital status, political or religious beliefs, family, social or cultural background, or sexual orientation, unfairly grant any advantage to any student." Ernie told Larry he had behaved appropriately in his class and it would be unreasonable for him to do anything except what he would do for any other student. Given his past behavior in the classroom, Larry would have to fail Dale for the grading period. Ernie promised to support him in the matter.

That night, Larry went over in his head his own teaching behavior, his attitudes about athletes, about black students, and about both Dale and Mr. Anderson. The more he thought, the less sure he was that he was completely free from biased or prejudiced behavior or attitudes in his classes. At the same time, Dale had been cheating, and in any other case he would fail the student. Finally, Larry decided that Ernie was right and he would have to accept the consequences of giving Dale a failing grade for the grading period.

The Case of Andrew McLaughlin

Jane Heugh has taught at Horace Mann for 5 years and is generally acknowledged to be one of the better teachers in the English department. She is popular with both the students and her colleagues and cares deeply about what happens to the students at Horace Mann. Although Jane has a great deal of respect for many of her colleagues, the teacher with whom she has worked the most during the past 5 years has been Andrew McLaughlin. Andrew has been a public school English teacher for 37 years and believes himself still to be in his prime. Although he no longer bothers with lesson plans, and uses the same handouts and tests that he was using when Jane started teaching, Andrew has repeatedly told Jane that he is as up-to-date and hard-working as he was when he began teaching. Unfortunately, Jane has begun to have more and more doubts about Andrew's competence. From her perspective, Jane believes that Andrew has simply decided to "retire in place" and has long since ceased to offer his students the quality of instruction to which Jane believes they are entitled.

Because of departmental politics, Jane has thus far kept her opinions to herself. After all, she has argued, she is not the person responsible for evaluating Andrew's performance, nor has she actually seen him teaching. She thinks that Andrew is outdated and out of touch, and very much doubts that the students in his classes learn very much, but isn't sure that this gives her the right (let along the duty) to make an issue of his competence. Despite her silence, Jane has become aware of a growing barrier between Andrew and herself and suspects that he must be cognizant of her concerns. She has discussed the situation with friends who teach at other schools, but has not mentioned her feelings to anyone at Horace Mann. Her friends at other schools have been sympathetic and have talked about similar situations in their own schools, but have advised her simply to wait out Andrew's retirement, which will, after all, come within the next few years. So, while she is bothered and annoyed by the situation, Jane has continued to keep her reservations to herself and avoid any direct confrontation with Andrew. She isn't happy with this solution, but can't think of any viable alternatives.

Analysis and Discussion. In each of the above four cases, an individual is presented with an ethical dilemma. The dilemmas are very different in terms of their subjects, their relative importance, and the ways in which they are resolved. Further, the ethical decisions made by the four individuals involved vary considerably with regard to the quality of the judgments made. However, all four cases share a number of common features as well, and we will begin by discussing these common features.

First of all, in each case there is in fact a real *dilemma* present. Very often, people talk about moral or ethical "dilemmas" in situations where most of us would have no problem at all deciding what to do. These are not actually dilemmas in any meaningful sense. A dilemma is an instance in which we do not wish to accept *any* of the possible options. In other words, a true dilemma exists only where we are choosing among undesirable choices. There are, in short, *no* "good" solutions or "right" answers; rather, there are only more or less "good" or "right" solutions. James Rafferty is torn between his obligations toward a student who may have been sexually harassed by a teacher and his feelings for his friend and colleague Dick Swenson. Similarly, Mary Andrews is torn between what she sees as both personal and professional obligations and a promise she made to her cooperating teacher. Larry Epstein is torn between his own professional standards (as well as the NEA "Code of Ethics for the Education Profession") and pressure from his principal. Finally, Jane Heugh is torn between her concerns about a colleague she believes to be no longer competent and her belief that his problems are really not her business. In other words, in each case presented here the central figure feels torn by conflicting obligations, desires, or beliefs.

Another common characteristic in each of these four cases is that each person attempts to discuss his or her ethical dilemma with another person to help clarify and resolve it. Further, with the exception of James Rafferty, each of educators involved has turned to one or more individuals outside the actual dilemma itself. Thus, Mary turns first to a friend and then her university supervisor. Larry Epstein, after his problematic meeting with the principal, went to his department chairperson, Ernie Smith, for advice. Jane Heugh has discussed her concerns with friends who teach at other schools. By discussing the dilemma that faces them with a presumably neutral third party, each of these three individuals has increased the likelihood of making a sound ethical judgment. In contrast, James Rafferty discusses his dilemma only with Dick Swenson—the key figure, in many ways, in the dilemma. As a consequence, he ends up making a judgment that most of us would consider highly questionable at best, and more probably downright unethical.

Further, in each of the four cases that we have examined, the individual involved did not rush to make a decision, but rather attempted to take a reasonable amount of time to make a sound and well-informed decision. While one may have reservations or even objections to the decisions that each of the four people made (as we ourselves do), it is clear that each one did in fact agonize about his or her dilemma and did try to resolve the dilemma in the best way that he or she could. In other words, all four individuals did actually engage, to some extent, in reflection about their ethical dilemmas. This is an important point because it reminds us that reflection, whatever its many benefits (and it *does* have many benefits, we believe), does not and cannot guarantee that our decisions and judgments will always be the right ones.

Last, these four cases make evident a claim offered some years ago by Richard Peters, a British philosopher of education, who argued that:

> [Today] there are no set systems of teaching and no agreed aims of education; there is constant controversy about the curriculum and a welter of disagreement about how children ought to be treated. In more settled times only the very reflective teacher was led to probe behind the tradition for a rationale for what [she or] he ought to do; nowadays it is only the lazy or dogmatic teacher who can avoid such

probing. Neither can the modern teacher find in the appeal
to authority much more than a temporary resting place; for
authorities disagree, and on what grounds is the advice of
one rather than another to be heeded? The unpalatable truth
is that the modern teacher has no alternative to thinking out
these matters for [herself or] himself. Teachers can no longer
be merely trained; they have also to be educated. (Peters,
1966, p. 23)

Ethics and ethical decision making, in short, are simply a part of
teaching, and the classroom teacher could no more ignore or avoid
ethical and moral dilemmas than she or he could avoid curricular or
methodological decisions. In each of the four cases presented above,
the ethical dilemma that occurs is brought about by factors largely
beyond the individual's control, and yet must be addressed by the
individual.

With these four cases in mind as background, we turn now to a
discussion of the relationship of opinions, preferences, and value
judgments as these affect moral and ethical decision making.

Opinions, Preferences, and Value Judgments

A very common view today voiced by educators and others in
our society is that all opinions are of equal weight, are equally valid,
and should be equally respected. Such a view is certainly tolerant
and no doubt well intentioned, but it is also, plain and simply,
wrong. If you think about this claim in the context of medicine, for
instance, you will see how absurd it really is. If I am suffering from
a particular illness, my grandmother, the mechanic who services my
car, and my physician may well all have opinions both about what
ails me and about what should be done for the ailment. While I love
my grandmother dearly, and while I both respect and trust my
mechanic, on medical matters it would not seem to be at all reasonable
for me to trust either of them instead of, or in place of, my physician.
Now, this does not mean that in a particular case one of them might
not be more correct than the physician—but the odds (as well as
human reason) would still suggest that I am better off to go with the

expert. As one humorous old saying goes, "The race is not always to the swift, nor the battle to the strong, but that's the way to bet." The same, of course, would apply to the building of a house, the repair of a car, or the best way to teach a particular topic in the classroom. In each instance, some individuals will have greater expertise, competence, and skill than will others, and it is only reasonable and appropriate to favor their opinions somewhat disproportionately. This does not mean that once we have identified the experts in a particular field, we automatically empower them to make decisions. The actual responsibility for the decision making rests with us; it is my health, my car, and my house about which I must make decisions. The same is true when we move from the arena of personal problems to social problems. As John Dewey explained:

> Inquiry, indeed, is a work which devolves upon experts. But their expertness is not shown in framing and executing policies, but in discovering and making known the facts upon which the former depend. They are technical experts in the sense that scientific investigators and artists manifest *expertise*. It is not necessary that the many should have the knowledge and skill to carry on the needed investigations; what is required is that they have the ability to judge of the bearing of the knowledge supplied by others upon common concerns. (Dewey, 1927, pp. 208-209)

When we turn to the area of ethical decisions and decision making, of course, the problem is in locating the experts. In fact, when we evaluate ethical or moral judgments and decisions, we do so not on the basis of expert opinion at all, but rather on the basis of the quality of reasoning and evidence that underlies the judgment or decision (see Becker, 1973). Thus, in the case of James Rafferty presented above, we might be very critical of both the evidentiary base on which his decision was made (which consisted, in essence, of Maria's word against Dick's word), as well as on the quality of the decision-making process itself, which allowed James to establish himself as both judge and jury in a case in which he had, to some extent, a vested interest. Another important aspect involved in evaluating ethical and moral judgments and decisions has to do with the type of claim that is actually being offered, and it is to a discussion of the differences between *preference claims* and *value judgments* that we now turn.

Very often in conversation and discussion we make two different types of claims that relate to ethical issues: preference claims and value judgments. Although both types of claims can be concerned with questions of right and wrong, proper and improper conduct, and so on, their logical status is quite different, and the two types of claims should not be used interchangeably. Preference claims are claims about what an individual speaker believes, prefers, wishes, and so forth. Thus, if I say, "I love chocolate," or "I don't believe that extramarital sex is moral," I am merely reporting on my own feelings about these matters. Such information may be interesting, or even important, for others to know and may help to explain my own behavior. However, since these are reports of my personal preferences, I am under no obligation to defend them, nor do I have to offer evidence or arguments on their behalf. If my friend Glenda were to announce that she did not like broccoli, she would be reporting on a personal preference. In such a context, judgments or claims of right and wrong are simply misguided. Glenda is neither right nor wrong to dislike broccoli; she simply doesn't like it, and that is all there is to the matter. Finally, the only way in which preference claims can be judged at all is in terms of how well they appear to reflect the reality of the individual speaker's preferences (see Riegle, Rhodes, & Nelson, 1990, p. 18; Wilson, 1967, pp. 56-74). In other words, given that Glenda has announced her dislike of broccoli, it is reasonable to assume that she would not go out of her way to order broccoli in restaurants, nor would she be likely to serve it frequently in her own home. If upon examination we discover that she has specifically ordered broccoli on numerous occasions, and further, that she often serves herself an especially generous helping, we would have reason to doubt that claim that she dislikes the vegetable (though there are, of course, other possible explanations as well).

Value judgments also report on ethical and moral (as well as aesthetic) matters, but unlike preference claims, they are public statements that seek to suggest that others ought to agree. Thus, a claim like, "Abortion is always, under all circumstances, wrong," is not a preference claim at all; rather, it is a value statement that entails the implicit claim that others ought to agree with the position the speaker is advocating. Since value statements are public in nature, evidence and arguments must be offered to support them, and they can (and should) be debated in the realm of public discourse and debate. Value judgments, in short, must be justified in some manner (see Riegle et al., 1990, p. 18; Wilson, 1967, pp. 56-74). However, it is important to note here that while it is true that value judgments must be justified, this does not mean that we will always be able to reach agreement about them. As John Wilson, the British philosopher of education, has quite correctly observed, "Unfortunately we do not always agree about the criteria of method of verification appropriate to our value statements" (Wilson, 1967, p. 66).

In the area of educational policy, many controversial matters are debated and argued about in various forums. For example, school prayer, school choice, sex education, merit pay for teachers, and a host of other curricular, methodological, and financial matters are all current topics of dispute that entail, at least in part, ethical and moral disagreements. In such debates and disputes, value judgments play a central role, as well they should. The underlying issues are often issues of value, and it is important that we, as a community, identify and debate these issues, recognizing from the outset that not everyone will agree with the final outcome. What we can do, however, is distinguish among personal preferences, value judgments, and empirical claims and respond to each type of claim appropriately. For instance, although personal preferences may well guide our individual feelings about these topics, we cannot in good conscience expect others to honor preference claims, since these are not public in nature. About value judgments, we can expect debate and sometimes disagreement among reasonable people. Finally, when we can reduce a debate to empirical claims (such as, "the distribution of condoms in secondary schools will result in a decrease in teen pregnancy"), then our debate moves from one of values to one in which resolution can be achieved without necessarily reaching an agreement on values. In short, the distinction between preference claims and value judgments, although a very significant one, is often glossed over or missed entirely in actual policy debates, and this may be one of the reasons that policies are often less clear, cogent, and reasonable than we might wish.

Competing Ethical Theories and the Educator

Another way in which ethical decision making can be approached is by examining the various ethical theories that have been proposed, defended, and critiqued historically by moral philosophers and ethicists. Among the most common ethical theories are utilitarianism, egoism, relativism, deontological theories, and so on (see Garner & Rosen, 1967; Riegle et al., 1990, pp. 55-57; Rosen, 1978). While the study of such ethical theories is both fascinating and worthwhile, a detailed treatment of each of these different approaches to ethical decision making is not possible here. Instead, all of these different ethical theories can be grouped together in two broad, general approaches—consequentialist ethical theories and non-consequentialist ethical theories—and we will limit our discussion to these two broad categories (see Strike, Haller, & Soltis, 1988; Strike & Soltis, 1992).

Consequentialist ethical theories, in essence, are theories that focus on the results of our actions in determining their rightness or wrongness. Thus, any particular action is neither intrinsically good nor intrinsically bad; rather, it is good or bad only in some context. On such an account, telling a lie might, in some cases, be the ethically correct course of action. For example, if you have a child in your class for whom you feel a certain antipathy (which, as a committed educator, you have naturally tried to control), and the child comes up to you one day and says, "You really don't like me, do you?" many teachers would agree that this is a case where telling a lie might be preferable to telling the truth. From a consequentialist perspective, one would be obligated to consider the results of one's actions, rather than looking at the actions in a context-free manner. Further, from a consequentialist perspective, "motives are not relevant to the rightness of actions but only to the goodness of persons" (Rosen, 1978, p. 99).

The best-known example of a consequentialist ethical theory is utilitarianism, which basically advocates that one should seek those policies and actions that will result in the "greatest good for the greatest number." Although such an approach has initial plausibility and appeal, you should be aware that in practice it can sometimes lead us to very strange, and morally problematic, outcomes. It is possible, for instance, to describe a situation in which a utilitarian approach would require us to argue that the establishment of a society based on human slavery might be an ethical option—an outcome with which most of us would have very serious problems. Similarly, as Strike and Soltis (1992) describe, a utilitarian approach could lead us to agree that torture might be morally acceptable:

> Let us imagine that a dozen sadistic people have had the good fortune to have captured a potential victim. They are debating whether or not it would be right to spend a pleasant evening torturing their captive. One of the group argues in the following way: "We must admit that by torturing this person we will cause a certain amount of pain. But think how much pleasure we will give ourselves. And there are a dozen of us. While this person's pain may exceed the pleasure of any one of us, it surely cannot exceed the pleasure of all of us. Thus, the average utility is enhanced by torturing this person. We ought to do so." (p. 14)

In short, if a utilitarian approach would lead to such outcomes, then we need to be very careful as we consider such approaches to ethics. Something, in short, seems to be very wrong.

Nonconsequentialist ethical theories constitute the other major category of ethical and moral theories. These theories presuppose some sort of universal moral or ethical principle or principles that should guide all behavior, regardless of the consequences of a particular action in a single context. Thus, if telling a lie is wrong, it must be wrong in all possible contexts. The Ten Commandments are, basically, an example of a nonconsequentialist ethical theory. God did not provide Moses with recommendations or suggestions; what the tablets contained were *commandments*. Thus, the commandment is "Thou shall not commit adultery," not "Thou shall not commit adultery, except where the other party is willing and you are unlikely to get caught." The NEA "Code of Ethics of the Education Profession," which was referred to in the case of Larry Epstein (and which is reprinted in Strike & Soltis, 1992, pp. ix-xi), also provides an example of a collection of principles that do not appear to allow for a great deal of situational flexibility—though they do provide a bit more flexibility than the Ten Commandments. Nonconsequentialist ethical theories entail three related features. Specifically,

1. The moral or ethical principle involved must be a genuine, universal principle.
2. The moral or ethical principle involved must be applied impartially; that is, it must apply to all people.
3. The moral or ethical principle must be applied consistently, and the related moral judgment involved in its application must be consistent. (Strike & Soltis, 1992, pp. 15-16)

As with the case of consequentialist ethical theories, so too with nonconsequentialist ethical theories are there some problems. Perhaps the most troubling aspect of most nonconsequentialist ethical theories has to do with where the universal principles come from. One can address this problem theologically, of course, as in the case of the Ten Commandments, but such an approach has limited force in a secular society. The German philosopher Immanuel Kant provided an alternative way of thinking about universal ethical principles, based on what he called the *categorical imperative.* In essence, the categorical imperative is the universal principle or rule by which one can test all other ethical or moral rules upon which one might take action. In other words, the idea underlying the categorical imperative is that ". . . the practical or moral law as such is strictly universal; universality being, as it were, its form. Hence all concrete principles of conduct must partake in this universality if they are to qualify for being called moral" (Copleston, 1960, p. 117). In any case, it is clear that we do not yet possess anywhere near a unanimity of opinion about the origin and nature of such universal principles, and this lack of unanimity is a serious problem for nonconsequentialist ethical theories. There is an additional problem here as well, since it is sometimes the case that two or more ethical principles on which we have reached agreement can, in actual practice, conflict.

This is a common problem with the NEA "Code of Ethics of the Education Profession," the Ten Commandments, and indeed any ethical code, as we shall see.

The Role of Reflection in Ethical Professional Practice

Given the above discussion of consequentialist and nonconsequentialist ethical theories, and their problems and limitations, what are we left with? Certainly we are left somewhat frustrated, and perhaps irritated, since it is clear that there are no easy solutions or techniques for resolving ethical dilemmas quickly and painlessly. At the same time, our discussion thus far should make clear why a chapter on ethics is necessary in a book concerned with reflective practice. Ethical decisions and decision making are inevitably a necessary part of teaching, as we have seen, and at the same time ethical decision making is as resistant to "cookbook" types of approaches as are other aspects of good teaching. In short, the same kinds of concerns and considerations that affect reflective practice in general will affect ethical decision making in particular.

Perhaps most important in making ethical and moral judgments in the classroom is the need to recognize that such judgments are not merely matters of personal opinion and preference; rather, they are judgments, and as such must be publicly defended and supported. Further, it is important to keep in mind that there is an critical difference in some cases between what the institutional rules and regulations (or even the law itself) dictate and what we may believe to be ethically or morally correct. The better our reasoning, the better our ethical decisions will be. This does not, of course, mean that all of our ethical decisions and judgments will be perfect, but it does mean that we will have done our best and have made the greatest possible use of the resources available to us in making our decisions and judgments. As Donald Vandenberg (1983) has argued:

> The ethical problems of educational practice ought therefore be reasoned through with as much objectivity as possible. This means that the questions of pedagogy should be

considered as moral questions and reasoned through in terms of universal obligations expressed as human rights. No ethical, political, social, religious, or psychological ideology should be imposed upon these educational questions, for these are manipulative, part of the problem, and an affront to human dignity. (p. 55)

In short, education is an endeavor that is intrinsically ethical in nature, and just as we wish to ensure that educators are competent masters of their subject matter, the pedagogical knowledge of their craft, and the actual methods to be used in the classroom, so too should we hope that they will be good ethical decision makers. Underlying all of these hopes, of course, is the goal of the reflective practitioner.

Propositions for Reflection and Consideration

1. Ethical decisions and judgments involve real dilemmas, in which one is presented with two or more undesirable options from which a choice must be made.
2. Good ethical decisions and judgments are the result of reflective interaction involving other people, preferably individuals not themselves involved in the ethical dilemma.
3. Not all opinions are of equal worth. Opinions must be judged by public criteria to determine their validity. To some extent, the opinion of an expert in his or her own field is likely to be of greater value than that of a nonexpert.
4. Personal preferences and value judgments are logically and practically distinct, and only the latter should be taken into account in deciding public matters and disputes (including those in the educational realm).
5. Ethical judgments and decisions may be based on either consequentialist or nonconsequentialist ethical theories, but in either case they must also rest on public evidence and argument.
6. Ultimately, ethical judgments and decisions must be held to the same standards of evidence and rationality as other types of judgments and decisions.

Toward Reflective Practice

Reflective teachers are never satisfied that they have all the answers. By continually seeking new information, they constantly challenge their own practices and assumptions. In the process new dilemmas surface and teachers initiate a new cycle of planning, acting, observing, and reflecting.

Dorene Ross, Elizabeth Bondy,
and Diane Kyle (1993, p. 337)

Okay, So What Now?

Deborah Jones is a first-year teacher at Willowsprings Elementary School. She recently graduated from Southern State College, where the teacher education program had emphasized the need for teachers to be more *reflective* in their teaching. Although she agreed with this goal, at least as far as she understood what it meant, Deborah really isn't at all sure how she should really go about trying to become more reflective. In preparing for the start of classes in September, Deborah spent the summer reviewing all of her old course notes and materials, and even reread some of her textbooks. She felt reasonably confident about her ability to teach the curriculum and, having had a fairly successful student teaching experience, also thought that she could handle classroom management and discipline issues, though these made her a bit more nervous than curricular issues. What she didn't know, she realized, was how to learn on the job—how to engage in the reflection that her professors had advocated. In fact, after looking through her notebooks, she realized that very little had been said in her courses about what reflection and reflective practice actually were, let alone how one could learn to embody them. So, she thought, what now?

Analysis and Discussion. Deborah's dilemma is far from uncommon. She is committed, in principle, to trying to become both a good teacher and a reflective teacher, but she isn't sure (a) what these terms really mean, and (b) how to go about becoming good and reflective. Thus far in *Becoming a Reflective Educator*, we have attempted to answer the first set of questions. By this point, you should have a fairly clear idea about what is meant by the term *reflective practitioner*, and should also understand how reflective practice is related to inquiry, to transformational curricula and instruction, to school leadership issues broadly conceived, to the social and communal nature of the schooling process, and to issues of professional ethics. In the remainder of this chapter, we will try to provide some guidelines and suggestions for educators who wish to become reflective practitioners.

Toward Reflective Practice

In the first chapter of this book, we suggested that the process by which one becomes reflective is similar in many ways to the description in the children's story *The Velveteen Rabbit* of the way in which toys can become "real." However, becoming a reflective educator does not just require that one endures, gets older, and (perhaps) starts to come apart at the seams as a result of being loved, but also involves an active commitment on the part of the educator to go beyond routine behaviors and patterns of day-to-day functioning. As the quote above suggests, the process of becoming a reflective practitioner is, at its heart, one with no end or termination. Rather, it is an ongoing commitment to growth, change, development, and improvement.

Reflective educators are constantly testing the assumptions and inferences they have made about their work as teachers. As Donald Schön (1983, 1987) has suggested, reflective practice is in essence a kind of "reflective conversation" involving the educator, students, parents, and other teachers. Educators need to realize that their actions as teachers take place in a context of meanings in which other participants have different interpretations and understandings (indeed, different constructions of reality). It is important that these different, and sometimes competing, interpretations, understandings, and constructions of reality be taken into account to as great an extent as possible by the reflective educator. For example, Deborah Jones might realize that her setting high academic standards for a particular child in her class could be in conflict with other standards to which the child is exposed in the course of his or her day. Deborah, in short, must reflect upon the limits of her influence as well as on her actions as a teacher.

In this chapter, as was suggested above, we will offer some suggestions to help you become increasingly reflective. Bear in mind, though, that there is no simple formula for success, nor is there any guaranteed way in which one can be totally assured of becoming a reflective educator—any more than there is a guaranteed method of becoming a good teacher.

The Reflective Journal

In an increasing number of pre-service teacher education programs, journal writing has become a very important practice. Pre-service teachers are often asked to write down their experiences at the end of a day of teaching, reflect upon them, draw conclusions from them, and share their insights about the day's events with their cooperating teacher as well as their university supervisor. Many effective teachers continue journal writing and reflection as regular classroom teachers. Sharing is done with other teachers, the principal, and others with whom the teachers have professional contact and in whom they have confidence. In addition, reflective journals can play an important role in analyzing significant social and educational issues that affect students and the learning environment.

Portraiture

Unfortunately, many teachers never share their instructional skills with other teachers because they decide to confine their creativity and insights to the isolation of their own classrooms. One way of addressing their problem is the process of *portraiture*, in which teams of teachers have the opportunity to observe each other, write portraits of what they have observed, and share their insights with the other team members (see Rogers & Brubacher, 1988). The process of portraiture is especially useful when kept clearly distinct from the formal process of teacher evaluation, though of course there is an obvious overlap between good, formative teacher evaluation and the goals and objectives of portraiture. This process allows teachers to focus on the nature of teaching and learning, as well as on their own teaching practice, in a reflective and constructive manner.

Professional Development

There are several ways in which school districts can use reflective practice to undergird, support, and motivate staff development. At Washington State University's "Project Learn," for example, teams of teachers define problems occurring in the classroom and then work together to develop and implement possible solutions. These solutions are shared with participating teachers and their school districts. A similar approach has been undertaken in Boston by the "Educator's Forum," where teachers are provided with the opportunity to inquire into the critical issues that confront them in their schools and classrooms. Both of these examples involve reflective practice, as well as collaborative interactions designed to address the real-world problems of classroom teachers.

Action Research

Action research projects, which encourage teachers to initiate inquiry into the problems that confront them in the classroom, are once again becoming an important feature of American education. Forty years ago action research was a powerful stimulus for change—indeed, it was important enough that at one point the Association for Supervision and Curriculum Development (ASCD) identified action research as an organizational objective. Action research, as discussed earlier in this book, can play an important role not only in the improvement of specific pedagogical practices, but also in the development of a culture of inquiry in the school and reflective educational practice on the part of the classroom teacher.

Journals, portraiture, professional development activities, and action research are a few of the many ways in which teachers and other educators can seek to become reflective practitioners. The biggest challenge facing Deborah Jones (and the rest of us), though, is actually deciding to make the commitment to become reflective educators. Once on the road to reflective practice, Deborah will find that there are many interesting and valuable paths that she can follow toward the goal of becoming increasingly reflective as a professional educator.

References

Accelerated Schools Project. (1991). Hollibrook Accelerated Elementary School. *Accelerated Schools, 1*(3), 4-9.

Apple, M. W., & Weiss, L. (Eds.). (1983). *Ideology and practice in schooling*. Philadelphia: Temple University Press.

Barnard, C. (1938). *Functions of the executive*. Cambridge, MA: Harvard University Press.

Barzun, J. (1954). *Teacher in America*. Garden City, NY: Doubleday.

Barzun, J. (1991). *Begin here: The forgotten conditions of teaching and learning*. Chicago: University of Chicago Press.

Becker, L. (1973). *On justifying moral arguments*. London: Routledge & Kegan Paul.

Berliner, D. (1986). In pursuit of the expert pedagogue. *Educational Researcher, 15*(7), 5-13.

Beyer, L. E., & Apple, M. W. (1988). *The curriculum: Problems, politics and possibilities*. Albany: State University of New York Press.

Bissex, G., & Bullock, R. (Eds.). (1987). *Seeing for ourselves: Case-study research by teachers of writing*. Portsmouth, NH: Heinemann.

Bogdan, R., & Biklen, S. (1992). *Qualitative research for education: An introduction to theory and methods*. Boston: Allyn & Bacon.

Bowers, C. A. (1984). *The promise of theory: Education and the politics of cultural change*. New York: Longman.

Boydston, J. A. (Ed.). (1970). *Guide to the works of John Dewey*. Carbondale: Southern Illinois University Press.

Boyer, E. (1983). *High school: A report on secondary education in America.* New York: Harper & Row.

Broudy, H. S. (1961). *Paradox and promise: Essays on American life and education.* Englewood Cliffs, NJ: Prentice-Hall.

Bullough, R. V., Jr. (1989). *First year teacher: A case study.* New York: Teachers College Press.

Burns, J. M. (1979). *Leadership.* New York: Harper & Row.

Callahan, R. E. (1962). *Education and the cult of efficiency: A study of the social forces that have shaped the administration of the public schools.* Chicago: University of Chicago Press.

Case, C., Lanier, J., & Miskel, C. (1986). The Holmes Group report: Impetus for gaining professional status for teachers. *Journal of Teacher Education, 37*(4), 36-43.

Case, C., & Olsen, P. (Eds.). (1974). *The future: Create or inherit.* Deans' Committee of the Study Commission on Undergraduate Education and the Education of Teachers. Lincoln: University of Nebraska.

Chambliss, J. (1987). *Educational theory as theory of conduct.* Albany: State University of New York Press.

Clabaugh, G. K., & Rozycki, E. G. (1990). *Understanding schools.* New York: Harper & Row.

Clark, E. (1983, October). The curious odyssey of Dr. Littky. *Yankee Magazine, 47*(10), 198-217.

Comer, J. (1980). *School power.* New York: Free Press.

Connelly, F., & Clandinin, D. (1990). Stories of experience and narrative inquiry. *Educational Researcher, 19*(5), 2-14.

Copleston, F. (1960). *A history of philosophy: Vol. 6. Modern philosophy, part II—Kant.* Garden City, NY: Image Books.

Counts, G. S. (1932). *Dare the schools build a new social order?* New York: John Day.

Demos, J. (1970). *A little commonwealth: Family life in Plymouth Colony.* New York: Oxford University Press.

Dewey, J. (1910). *How we think.* Boston: D.C. Heath.

Dewey, J. (1927). *The public and its problems.* New York: Henry Holt.

Dewey, J. (1933). *How we think: A restatement of the relations of reflective thinking to the educative process* (2nd rev. ed.). Lexington, MA: D.C. Heath.

Dewey, J. (1938). *Logic: The theory of inquiry.* New York: Henry Holt.

Dewey, J. (1943). *The child and the curriculum/The school and society*. Chicago: University of Chicago Press. (Original works published 1902 and 1900)

Dewey, J. (1944). *Democracy and education: An introduction to the philosophy of education*. New York: Free Press. (Original work published 1916)

Dewey, J. (1948). *Reconstruction in philosophy* (Enlarged ed.). Boston: Beacon.

Dewey, J. (1975). *Moral principles in education*. Carbondale: Southern Illinois University Press. (Original work published 1909)

Dewey, J. (1976). The relationship of thought and its subject matter. Reprinted in J. Boydston (Ed.), *John Dewey: The middle works: Vol. 2 (1902-1903)* (pp. 298-315). Carbondale: Southern Illinois University Press. (Original work published 1903)

Dewey, J. (1979). Contributions to *A cyclopedia of education*. Reprinted in J. Boydston (Ed.), *John Dewey: The middle works: Vol. 7 (1912-1914)* (pp. 207-366). Carbondale: Southern Illinois University Press. (Original work published 1912-1913)

Dewey, J., & Dewey, E. (1962). *Schools of tomorrow*. New York: E. P. Dutton. (Original work published 1915)

Dykhuizen, G. (1973). *The life and mind of John Dewey*. Carbondale: Southern Illinois University Press.

Eisner, E. (1982). *Cognitive and curriculum: A basis for deciding what to teach*. New York: Longman.

Eisner, E. W., & Vallance, E. (1974). *Conflicting conceptions of curriculum*. Berkeley, CA: McCutchan.

Feyerabend, P. (1978). *Against method: Outline of an anarchistic theory of knowlege*. London: Verso.

Fine, M. (1991). *Framing dropouts: Notes on the politics of an urban public high school*. Albany: State University of New York Press.

Fitzgibbons, R. (1981). *Making educational decisions: An introduction to philosophy of education*. New York: Harcourt Brace Jovanovich.

Fosnot, C. (1989). *Enquiring teachers, enquiring learners: A constructivist approach to teaching*. New York: Teachers College Press.

Fraenkel, J., & Wallen, N. (1990). *How to design and evaluate research in education*. New York: McGraw-Hill.

Freire, P. (1972). *Pedagogy of the oppressed*. New York: Herder and Herder.

Freud, T. (1986). The passion of Dennis Littky. *New England Monthly*, *3*(9): 44-48, 76-78, 117-119.

Gage, N. L. (1978). *The scientific basis of the art of teaching*. New York: Teachers College Press.

Gage, N. L. (1985). *Hard gains in the soft sciences: The case of pedagogy*. Bloomington, IN: Phi Delta Kappa.

Gardner, J. W. (1990). *On leadership*. New York: Free Press.

Garner, R., & Rosen, B. (1967). *Moral philosophy: A systematic introduction to normative ethics and meta-ethics*. New York: Macmillan.

Geertz, C. (1973). *The interpretation of cultures*. New York: Basic Books.

Geertz, C. (1983). *Local knowledge: Further essays in interpretive anthropology*. New York: Basic Books.

Gehrke, N. J., Knapp, M. S., & Sirotnik, K. A. (1992). In search of the school curriculum. In G. Grant (Ed.), *Review of research in education: 18* (pp. 51-110). Washington, DC: American Educational Research Association.

Giroux, H. A. (1992). Educational leadership and the crisis of democratic government. *Educational Researcher, 21*(4): 8-11.

Giroux, H., & McClaren, P. (1989). *The curriculum: Problems, politics and possibilities*. Albany: State University of New York Press.

Glickman, C. D. (1989). *Supervision of instruction*. Needham Heights, MA: Allyn & Bacon.

Goodlad, J. I. (1984). *A place called school*. New York: McGraw-Hill.

Goodlad, J. I., & Associates. (1979) *Curriculum inquiry: The study of curriculum practice*. New York: McGraw-Hill.

Goodlad, J. I., Soder, R., & Sirotnik, K. A. (Eds.). (1990). *The moral dimension of teaching*. San Francisco: Jossey-Bass.

Goswami, D., & Stillman, P. (Eds.). (1987). *Reclaiming the classroom: Teacher research as an agency for change*. Portsmouth, NH: Heinemann.

Green, T. (1971). *The activities of teaching*. New York: McGraw-Hill.

Green, T. (1985). The formation of conscience in an age of technology. *American Journal of Education, 94*(1), 1-32.

Hamm, C. (1989). *Philosophical issues in education: An introduction*. New York: Falmer Press.

Hammersley, M. (1990). *Reading ethnographic research: A critical guide*. London: Longman.

Hammersley, M. (1992). *What's wrong with ethnography? Methodological explorations*. London: Routledge.

Highet, G. (1950). *The art of teaching*. New York: Vintage.

Holmes Group, The. (1990). *Tomorrow's schools: Principles for the design of professional development schools*. East Lansing, MI: Author.

Hoy, W. K., & Miskel, C. (1987). *Educational administration: Theory, research and practice*. New York: Random House.

Illich, I. (1970). *Deschooling society*. New York: Harper & Row.

Illich, I. (1975). *Medical nemesis: The expropriation of health*. London: Calder & Boyars.

Irwin, J. (1987). *What is a reflective/analytical teacher?* Unpublished manuscript, University of Connecticut, School of Education.

Jackson, P. W. (1968). *Life in classrooms*. New York: Holt, Rinehart & Winston.

Jaeger, R. M. (Ed.). (1988). *Complementary methods for research in education*. Washington, DC: American Educational Research Association.

Jones, J. (1981). *Bad blood: The Tuskegee syphilis experiment—A tragedy of race and medicine*. New York: Free Press.

Kalwans, H. L. (1990). *Newton's madness: Further tales of clinical neurology*. New York: Harper & Row.

Kemmis, S., & McTaggart, R. (Eds.). (1988). *The action research planner* (3rd ed.). Victoria, Australia: Deakin University Press.

Kerlinger, F. N. (1973). *Foundational behavioral research* (2nd ed.). New York: Holt, Rinehart & Winston.

Killion, J., & Todnem, G. (1991). A process for personal theory building. *Educational Leadership, 48*(6), 14-16.

Kogelman, S., & Warren, J. (1978). *Mind over math*. New York: McGraw-Hill.

Kosinski, Jerzy. (1980). *Being There*. New York: Bantam.

Leinhardt, G. (1990). Capturing craft knowledge in teaching. *Educational Researcher, 19*(2), 18-25.

Leming, J. S. (1992). The influence of contemporary issues curricula on school aged youth. In G. Grant (Ed.), *Review of research in education: 18* (pp. 111-161). Washington, DC: American Educational Research Association.

Levin, H. (1991). Accelerated visions. *Accelerated Schools, 1*(3), 2-3.

Lincoln, Y., & Guba, E. (1985). *Naturalistic inquiry.* Beverly Hills, CA: Sage.

Ludmerer, K. (1985). *Learning to heal: The development of American medical education.* New York: Basic Books.

McLaren, P. (1989). *Life in schools.* New York: Longman.

Mezirow, J., & Associates. (1990). *Fostering critical thinking in adulthood.* San Francisco: Jossey-Bass.

Mohr, M., & MacLean, M. (1987). *Working together: A guide for teacher-researchers.* Urbana, IL: National Council of Teachers of English.

Morgenbesser, S. (Ed.). (1977). *Dewey and his critics: Essays from the journal of philosophy.* New York: The Journal of Philosophy.

Oakes, J. (1985). *Keeping track: How schools structure inequality.* New Haven, CT: Yale University Press.

Perkinson, H. J. (1993). *Teachers without goals, students without purposes.* New York: McGraw-Hill.

Peters, R. S. (1966). *Ethics and education.* Glenview, IL: Scott, Foresman.

Pinar, W. F., & Reynolds, W. M. (Eds.). (1992). *Understanding curriculum as phenomenological and deconstructed text.* New York: Teachers College Press.

Pratte, R. (1977). *Ideology and education.* New York: David McKay.

Reagan, T. (1980). The foundations of Ivan Illich's social thought. *Educational Theory, 30*(4), 293-306.

Riegle, R., Rhodes, D., & Nelson, T. (1990). *The language and logic of educational policy* (2nd ed.). Lexington, MA: Ginn.

Robertson, E. (1992). Is Dewey's educational vision still viable? In G. Grant (Ed.), *Review of research in education: 18* (pp. 335-381). Washington, DC: American Educational Research Association.

Rogers, V., & Brubacher, J. (1988). Teacher portraiture: A timely proposal for more effective teacher development. *Journal of Personnel Evaluation in Education, 1*: 245-257.

Rosen, B. (1978). *Strategies of ethics.* Boston: Houghton Mifflin.

Ross, D., Bondy, E., & Kyle, D. (1993). *Reflective teaching for student empowerment: Elementary curriculum and methods.* New York: Macmillan.

Sarason, S. (1990). *The predictable failure of educational reform.* San Francisco: Jossey-Bass.

Schön, D. (1983). *The reflective practitioner: How professionals think in action.* New York: Basic Books.

Schön, D. (1987). *Educating the reflective practitioner.* San Francisco: Jossey-Bass.

Schwab, J. (1970). *The practical: A language for curriculum.* Washington, DC: National Education Association.

Schwab, J. (1978). The practical: A language for curriculum. In I. Westbury & N. Wilkof (Eds.), *Joseph Schwab: Science, curriculum, and liberal education* (pp. 287-321). Chicago: University of Chicago Press.

Sherman, R., & Webb, R. (Eds.). (1988a). *Qualitative research in education: Focus and methods.* London: Falmer Press.

Sherman, R., & Webb, R. (1988b). Qualitative research in education: A focus. In R. Sherman & R. Webb (Eds.), *Qualitative research in education* (pp. 1-21). London: Falmer Press.

Shulman, L. (1987). Knowledge and teaching: Foundations of the new reform. *Harvard Educational Review, 57*(1), 1-22.

Silberman, C. (1971). *Crisis in the classroom.* New York: Random House.

Sizer, T. (1984). *Horace's compromise: The dilemma of the American high school.* Boston: Houghton Mifflin.

Slavin, R. E. (1990). *Cooperative learning: Theory, research and practice.* Englewood Cliffs, NJ: Prentice-Hall.

Smyth, J. (1992). Teachers' work and the politics of reflection. *American Educational Research Journal, 29*(2), 267-300.

Soltis, J. F. (Ed.). (1987). *Reforming teacher education.* New York: Teachers College Press.

Sparks-Langer, G., & Colton, A. (1991). Synthesis of research on teachers' reflective thinking. *Educational Leadership, 48*(6), 37-44.

Spradley, J. (1980). *Participant observation.* New York: Holt, Rinehart & Winston.

Starr, P. (1982). *The social transformation of American medicine.* New York: Basic Books.

Stevens, R. (1983). *Law school: Legal education in America from the 1850s to the 1980s.* Chapel Hill: University of North Carolina Press.

Strike, K., Haller, E., & Soltis, J. (1988). *The ethics of school administration.* New York: Teachers College Press.

Strike, K., & Soltis, J. (1992). *The ethics of teaching* (2nd ed.). New York: Teachers College Press.

Teal, S., & Reagan, G. (1973). Educational goals. In J. Frymier (Ed.), *A school for tomorrow* (pp. 37-84). Berkeley, CA: McCutchan.

Tesconi, C. (1975). *Schooling in America: A social philosophical perspective*. Boston: Houghton Mifflin.

Tom, A. (1984). *Teaching as a moral craft*. New York: Longman.

Totten, W. F. (1970). *The power of community education*. Midland, MI: Pendell.

Toulmin, S. (1968). *An examination of the place of reason in ethics*. Cambridge, UK: Cambridge University Press.

Tozer, S., Violas, P., & Senese, G. (1993). *School and society: Educational practice as social expression*. New York: McGraw-Hill.

Vandenberg, D. (1983). *Human rights in education*. New York: Philosophical Library.

Van Doren, M. (1959). *Liberal education*. Boston: Beacon.

Van Manen, J. (1977). Linking ways of knowing with ways of being practical. *Curriculum Inquiry, 6*, 205-208.

Weiss, L. (Ed.). (1988). *Class, race and gender in American education*. Albany: State University of New York Press.

Westbrook, R. B. (1991). *John Dewey and American democracy*. Ithaca, NY: Cornell University Press.

Whyte, W. (Ed.). (1991). *Participatory action research*. Newbury Park, CA: Sage.

Williams, M. (1981). *The velveteen rabbit, or, how toys become real*. Philadelphia, PA: Running Press.

Wilson, J. (1967). *Language and the pursuit of truth*. Cambridge, UK: Cambridge University Press.

Zeichner, K., & Liston, D. (1987). Teaching student teachers to reflect. *Harvard Educational Review, 57*, 23-48.

Index